HAPPILY EVER AFTER

A Story of Reflection, Releasing and Rebuilding after a Failed Marriage

JENNIFER L. SPEED

1

Happily Ever After

Published in the United States of America

Acknowledgements

Thank you to my children, Skyla and Scottie Speed. All that I do is for you and through you I found incredible strength. You make my heartbeat. Thank you Jesus for my bounce back, resilience and restoring my peace of mind. I cannot thank my parents, David and Laurie Foster, enough for always being there for me and my children. Nothing was ever too grand for you to handle. I appreciate all that you have ever done for my family. An extra special thank you to my father for instilling in me the power of positivity. Thank you to my mother in love, Beverly Speed, for always remaining prayerful and for always being there for me and my children. I could not have asked for more. Thank you to my father in love, Allison Speed, for making my children's education a priority. Thank you to my cousins, Reese and Kasha Giddins, for all of your support and wisdom. Kasha, you remained steady every day while I wavered. Thank you for keeping me on my feet. Reese, your knowledge kept my house standing. The love and care from the two of you is golden. Thank you, Tiffany Williams, for picking up the phone and listening no matter how many times I called you. Thank you, Contessa Metcalfe, for planting the idea of writing this book and thank you to T. Makeda Leary for encouraging me to write it. Thank you, Monica Jenkins, for keeping the spark of writing ignited. Thank you to the rest of, who I refer to as, my army of friends for lending me your shoulders to lean on as I tumbled through the road of divorce; Latoya Anderson for sharing your experiences, Denean McArthur for always keeping me laughing, Melissa Dinas for always offering your time, Vicki Hadley for your constant support, Cornelius Jenkins for sharing your perspectives and Tawanna Simmons for all of your prayers. Thank you to my brother, Jarrett Foster, and his fiancé, Funmi Adigun, for always making sure my mind was occupied. Thank you, Gabriel Wallace, for your wisdom and for publishing my first book. Thank you, Carie Gardner and Phillip Gilliam, for being my sounding board. In some way, each of you has touched me and added incredible value to my life. Thank you just isn't enough...

Table of Contents

Chapter 1

In the Beginning

"Will you, Jason, have Vanessa to be your wife? Will you love her, comfort and keep her, and forsaking all others and remain true to her as long as you both shall live?"

"I will," Jason replied.

"With this ring I thee wed, and all my worldly goods I thee endow. In sickness and

in health, in poverty or in wealth, 'til death do us part."

And the pastor addressed the congregation, "Haven't you read," he said, "that at the

beginning the Creator 'made them male and female, and said, 'For this reason a

man will leave his father and mother and be united to his wife, and the two

will become one flesh? So, they are no longer two, but one flesh. "Therefore, what God has joined together, let no one separate."
Matthew 19:4-6

And just like that, we were one!

We were young, happy, blissful, and head over heels in love. We were going to build a family, laugh hard, love hard, travel the world together, and leave a legacy for our children. We had an amazing time doing that until he said, "I want to have an open marriage."

And then we became part of the statistics that 40-50% of all marriages end in divorce.

Join me as I tell a story of unspeakable joy, love, like, confusion, hurt, pain and back to happiness.

"Eric, hook me up with one of your boys," I said.

Eric was a really good friend that I met while we attended Temple University. We maintained a great friendship well beyond college years. He'd gone on to getting married to his soulmate, Kris, and I was still trying to find the right person. It was nearing time to take my nursing boards and I had just turned 25 years old. I was tired of dating just for the heck of it and wanted something more stable. I had a lot of respect for Eric and I knew that he wouldn't steer me wrong with a hook up.

"You should meet my cousin, Jason. He's from Philly but he lives in Wilkes Barre, about two hours away. He's getting his master's degree and he's a real good dude. I think you two would be equally yoked," he said.

"Cool! When can we meet?" I asked.

"He'll be at our house warming next week. I'll tell him about you," he said.

The next week I drove to Eric and Kris' house warming with great anticipation. I couldn't wait to meet this cousin of his. All of the guests sat around and were chatty but I didn't notice anyone that was looking for me. Eric and Kris were busy entertaining the entire time so it wasn't until the end of the party that I got a chance to talk with Eric. "Where's your cousin?" I asked.

He pointed to a slender handsome guy sitting across the room from me. He stood 6-foot 1 inch with creamy caramel colored skin. He had a very low even haircut and a clean shaved face. His eyebrows were somewhat bushy with puppy dog eyes. He had cute freckles on his nose and nice thick lips. He looked very serious, like he was in deep thought. He was quiet during the entire night. I initially decided that he wasn't the one for me but I figured I'd meet him anyway since that was the plan.

Eric introduced us and we talked for about twenty minutes. In that short time I learned that he owned a clothing store, mentored a young boy, and he loved his mom. I still wasn't impressed because he was too quiet. Opposite of him, I was very talkative. So when he walked me to my car and asked for my number I told him that I don't give out my number but I'll call him. He accepted that and we parted ways.

As Jason and I drove down the interstate I called my friend and told her about him. He and I were driving side by side when I waved to him, laughed and told her, "I'm never calling him."

Two months went by and Eric inquired about when I was going to call Jason. I told him, "I'm not going to call him. He's too young and too quiet."

"You need to let go of some of your rules Vanessa. He's a really good guy with a good head on his shoulders. He is younger than you but he's mature," he stated.

He and I went back and forth over the phone about this for thirty minutes until I finally said, "If I call him will you leave me alone about this?"

Confidently he said, "Yes!"

The next day I called him, and Eric was right. We did have a lot of things in common. We talked for two and a half hours about everything. By the end of the conversation I was 'in like' with Jason. I couldn't wait to see him and all I kept thinking about was the great conversation that we had.

A few days later he asked me to be his date at his friend's wedding. I said yes without hesitation and we were inseparable from that moment on.

Only a few months into dating I met his mom, Mimi. One of the first things she said to me was, "You look so much like his sister."

Jason had a sister, but she wasn't talking about her. She was saying I looked just like him. I guess she was right because from then on, we never stopped hearing that comment. We heard it so much that we knew when someone was going to say it and we would beat them by saying in unison, "We know. We look like brother and sister."

My skin complexion was slightly lighter than his and I had thin kissable lips in comparison to the fullness of his. My eyebrows were once thick like his but I wore them thin and arched. If you looked close enough I had dimples in my cheeks when I smiled.

10

My hair was straight and laid somewhere between past my shoulders and in the middle of my back. I was cute but with the right set of earrings, a sexy outfit and some lip gloss, I was fly.

I stood 5 foot 4 with an athletic build and thick runner's thighs with strong calves. I didn't have many curves but I had something even better, a beautiful personality. I was very bubbly and jovial on most days. It was rare to catch me having a bad day. I was very laid back and had a lot of growth under my belt so I hardly ever raised my voice. If I was out of character that meant someone had really crossed the line. Nothing made me happier than to be laughing and joking with friends and family.

Which was the one issue that I had with him. He didn't laugh or joke much, so one day I inquired, "Why are you so serious? You don't laugh much."

I don't know if he was waiting for an invitation or what but from there on we laughed, liked, and learned more about each other. About a year and a half into our courting we were in my apartment, laying on the bed underneath the fan when he said, "I think I love you."

"You think you do?" I inquired as my heart was racing.

"I love you Vanessa," he proclaimed.

11

I knew that I loved him but I wasn't about to be the first one to say it. "I love you too Jason," I happily responded.

Life was wonderful. It was like a fairytale. I had met the perfect mate for me and could not see myself going a single day without him. We went on vacations together, started a business, sort of adopted a teenager (not the brightest thing we ever did), and shared our dreams and aspirations with one another. On January 1, 2006, three and a half years after that two-and-a-half-hour conversation, our lives changed forever.

We were at a wedding reception and he told me that after the best man addresses the newly married couple he was going to take the mic and congratulate them also. About ten minutes into the New Year he said his congratulations and then called me to the front of the party. I was on the phone with my mother when he got on one knee and spoke clear into the mic, "Vanessa, will you marry me?"

Without hesitation I declared, "Yes!"

He was still on one knee and the ring was in the box when I bent over to hug him. I was elated and by the sounds of the screams coming through the phone, so was my mother. I put the phone to my ear and I heard her say, "Cal! I think Jason just proposed!"

I later found out that Jason asked my father for my hand in marriage the week before when we visited them for Christmas. He couldn't wait to welcome Jason into our family.

After I got off the phone we hugged and kissed and hugged and kissed and hugged and kissed some more. Everything was perfect. We consummated our engagement later that night and we fell asleep holding hands with the engagement ring shining bright.

I grew up in a household of four, my mother, father and brother, Rennie. My father was a very successful business man who taught us that we should be our own boss. We weren't rich but we had more than most people and my parents never struggled financially. My mother always put our family first. She would bend over backwards for us and walk a thousand miles if she had to. No union is perfect so I watched my parents go through the inevitable trials of marriage all while never missing a beat as they raised us. They both had much love for each other and finished on top by staying married until this day.

As a young woman approaching my mid-twenties, I wondered would I find a husband perfect for me. One who would love me and honor me and always put me first. I believed in true long-lasting love. One in which we supported each other's endeavors, shared our dreams and our insecurities without fear of judgement. We would raise a family of two or three children and build a legacy for them. We would own financially successful businesses that could be passed down to our children. We would conquer the world together and no man or woman could penetrate our bond. And then one day when we were hitting our 100's we would die together in bed holding hands. That's how I saw it.

Shortly after Jason proposed, Mimi shared a conversation with me that he had with her. He told her all of the reasons that he wanted to marry me and this one stood out. He said that I was perfect for him because I believed in him and I let him be who he is. It meant so much to him that I allowed him to dream and that I supported his aspirations. He had lofty business goals and he knew that I was the one that would allow him to follow his dreams. And he was right, because I came from a father who was given the freedom by his wife to build his dream. I saw some of my father in him and I believed in and admired him for his big vision.

I couldn't wait to become his wife and I felt like I had a bonus because of the way that he loved his mom. He wasn't a mama's boy but he always looked out for her and made sure she was well taken care of. His parents had a rather unusual union that ended in divorce after four children. Growing up, his parents never lived together but his dad would come to their home every day and check on them while handing out discipline when necessary. Jason didn't see many successful marriages and said that he had a hesitation to get married because he never wanted to hurt anyone. However, as we grew from like to love, he said that I deserved to be married and he couldn't wait to marry me, start a family and build an empire. So, knowing all of that, I figured he would never be the one to do me wrong, be unfaithful or break my heart. I knew that I had found the one.

On May 5th we were married on a beautiful spring day in Florida. Neither of us had wedding jitters. We knew that we wanted to spend the rest of our lives together and could not wait for it to be official.

As I entered the sanctuary, all of our family and friends rose from their seats. There was a white carpet rolled out for me in the aisle with perfectly scattered cream-colored rose petals. At the front of the room Jason waited for me with a calm cool smile on his face. He was so handsome.

Eric was his best man and stood amongst the groomsmen all dressed in light grey suits. The color complimented the maid of honor and bridesmaid's teal colored dresses.

There were two pillars each with a bundle of calla lilies behind each party and a beautifully decorated wedding arch full of roses and calla lilies. Beyond that was a huge window that gave way to a perfect view of the golf course that surrounded a large lake.

I walked down the aisle in total bliss to the Alicia Keys' song, 'If I Ain't Got You'. I saw one of my friends wipe away a tear and it made me get choked up. I didn't want any tears to fall so I sucked it up and chuckled to myself. Seeing everyone smile and stare made me feel like I needed to greet them so I smiled, waved my hand and pleasantly said, "Hello everybody."

The entire audience laughed and the ice was broken. That was so typical of me.

As the ceremony unfolded we held hands and smiled at each other. I kept trying to whisper things to him because I was so giddy with emotion. I was complete without Jason but with him I was unstoppable.

The ceremony was brief and then it was time to party. Everyone danced and ate all night. Halfway through the night my father made the most touching speech. He began to reminisce about me growing up and how bright my future was. He said he always thought there was no man good enough for me until he met Jason. "I liked all of Vanessa's boyfriends. They were nice but I love Jason," he said.

The audience clapped and Jason and I looked at each other and smiled. My father truly did love Jason and he treated him as if he was his son. He knew that Jason was right for me and would always do right by me.

Chapter 2

Our New Life Together

A few months after getting married we moved from the outskirts of Philadelphia to the suburbs of Atlanta. We bought a brand-new house and were well on our way to becoming a power couple. We still had a business together but decided to get jobs while the business grew. He got a job as a third-grade school teacher and I started working at the Children's Hospital. On my third day of orientation we got the best news that a couple could hear. I was pregnant! We couldn't be more ecstatic.

Nine months flew by and we celebrated our second wedding anniversary and nine days later, on my birthday, Joi came into the world. What a blessing she was! We had so much fun with her. I didn't know that I could love another being the way that I loved her. She was such a jewel. I wanted to be the best mommy that I could ever be for her and provide an incredible life for her. I really wanted to be a stay at home mom but financially we couldn't make that work.

Jason and I continued to be each other's best friends. We didn't just marry and then stop making each other happy. We dated each other. Did special things for one another. We truly liked each other, which, for us, was just as important as loving each other.

He knew that I loved surprises and so one day he surprised me by waking me early one morning and telling me that we were going to spend the day in the city. My bags were already packed and he'd set the day up so that every new destination was a surprise. That day I smiled so much that my cheeks hurt. We ended the night in a hotel downtown with me thanking him for a fantastic day.

I am very competitive and wanted to top Jason's surprise for me so when the Dallas Cowboys built a new stadium I knew exactly what my surprise to him would be. Jason was an avid football fan and on his bucket list was going to the new "state of the art" Dallas Cowboys' stadium. He was a diehard Eagles football fan. So, I figured I'd give him the surprise of a lifetime of watching the Eagles play in the Cowboys' stadium.

I was so full of eagerness to reveal my surprise that I avoided conversation with him the day before just so I wouldn't slip with the secret. We were leaving on Saturday so I was glad that he was out with his friends the night before. I packed our clothes and took the luggage to my parents' house so that there would be no chance of him finding it. My plan was to tell him that I was called into work Saturday morning so that I could get out the house early in the morning and be at the airport before he arrived. To get him to the airport his mom asked him to take her there so that she could fly to Philly. It was a perfect plan and I couldn't wait to execute it.

Saturday morning my alarm went off and I quickly hopped in the shower. I didn't want him to wake up and start talking to me because I was afraid I'd give it away. After showering I left without saying a word. I didn't even kiss him which was not like me at all. I drove away from the house feeling super giddy about what was about to unfold.

I was headed to my parents' house when he called me. I immediately got nervous and felt like he knew that I was up to something. I couldn't answer the phone so I just let it ring. Rennie was at my parents' house so that he could record Jason's reaction. I lived for this stuff, making my husband happy.

My mother drove us to the airport and during the ride my phone rang. Jason was calling. "Oh no! It's Jason again!" I said super giddy.

"Well answer the phone," my mother said.

"I can't he's gonna know," I refused.

He hung up and called right back. "He's calling again," I said as my palms started to sweat.

"Answer the phone. That man is worried about you," she demanded.

"Hello," I said making myself sound as if I was in a rush.

"Hey I've been calling you," he said sounding worried.

I didn't know what to say so I told the quickest lie that I could think of and said, "My phone fell between the seats and then I was late to work so I had to hurry up and get out the car so I didn't have time to call you back. And I'm in the middle of doing something right now so I can't talk."

"Ok. I just wanted to make sure everything was ok. You didn't say bye when you left and you didn't give me a kiss," he said.

"Oh, I'm sorry. I have to go. I'll call you when I'm done," I said very hurriedly and I hung up.

By now Rennie and I were at the airport and just waiting for Mimi's arrival. She called me when she was two minutes away from the terminal and pretended to be talking to someone else. That was my cue that she was near.

Jason pulled up to the curve and Rennie and I came running out from the terminal towards the car. I opened Jason's car door and said innocently but with a devious smile, "What are you doing here?"

He was genuinely confused and didn't know what to make of the situation. He asked me back, "What are you doing here?"

"I don't know. What are you doing here?" I responded playfully.

He just sat there dumbfounded with a confused grin on his face.

"Oh yeah. Here," I said and I handed him a small colorful gift bag with blue tissue paper sticking out.

He looked at me and said nothing as he accepted the bag. Shaking his head back and forth he cautiously peered into the bag. "Dallas Cowboy tickets?! Nah," he said shaking his head back and forth. He was still looking down at the tickets.

"Ok. Then I'll go by myself," I said smiling from ear to ear. I was grinning so much that my face hurt.

Two year old Joi was sitting in the back seat and was awakened by the commotion. She rubbed her eyes and said, "Hi Mommy."

I responded with a quick, "Good morning," and then turned my attention back to Jason.

"We're really going to the Cowboys stadium?" He asked again in total awe.

"No. It's just a joke. Let's all go back home," I quipped.

"No way!" he said rubbing his forehead.

"You alright in there?" Rennie chimed in.

"I saw you running across the street with that camera and I didn't know what was going on," he said to Rennie.

"You got him Vanessa," Mimi chimed in as she pumped her fists in the air.

"You got me," Jason sighed.

"Well let's go," I cheerfully said.

He got out the car and we both kissed Joi then said all of our goodbyes to the helpers and off we went to Dallas.

That was hands down one of the best highlights of our friendship called a marriage.

Chapter 3

The Writing on the Wall

Four years and sixteen days after Joi was born, Reese came into the world. He was another blessing because we tried two and a half years to conceive him. Life was great and I was living the dream. I had a boy and a girl and the love of my life at my side. But then everything came to a screeching halt the day before Thanksgiving 2012. Reese was only six months old and I was trying to get myself back into shape. Jason and I worked out early in the morning together before work. On this particular morning when the workout was complete and we were sitting on the floor trying to get enough energy to get ready for the day, he said, "I have to tell you something."

That sounded serious and I got a little nervous when I said, "What's that?"

He had an uncomfortable smirk on his face as he said, "I think I want to have sex with other people."

I was completely taken aback and shocked with what he said. I didn't know where this was coming from and I didn't know how to respond. At first, I said nothing and then I said, "Ok. Thank you for telling me."

That's just what I needed to get up off the floor and get myself dressed for work.

That evening after returning home from work neither of us addressed it and we just ended the night early. The next day we were at my parents' house amongst a house full of family and I had nothing to say. What was there to say? I was so confused because everything had been so perfect.

"What's wrong?" he asked me midway through the day.

I just looked at him, absent of words.

"You're upset because of yesterday?" he asked.

I looked to the ground and answered, "Yes."

"I understand. I'm not going to do it. I just wanted to tell you how I felt," he assured me.

That made me feel a little better but my feelings were still hurt and I was still so confused. Reese never slept more than 3 hours at a time and I was breast feeding him so I was always tired. Way too tired to have sex as frequently as we used to but I figured he would understand that with a new baby and all.

Somehow, we moved past that but it reappeared the following January. He again told me that he wanted to have sex with other people and I told him we needed to go to counseling. He agreed so we started carrying Reese with us to counseling every week for the next 4 weeks or so.

In counseling, he spoke of wanting to always have sex and never feeling satisfied. I immediately took ownership of the problem because we were only having sex maybe three or four times a month. Before having Reese, we had sex, on average, twice a week and sometimes three times. I realized that this was my fault and I had to get back to sex like it used to be.

In counseling, he also said that at work all of the women complimented how well he dressed and told him how handsome he was. He said I didn't compliment him enough. I wasn't owning that one and I said, "Why do I need to compliment you when you constantly tell me how handsome you look before I even have a chance to say anything?"

He understood where I was coming from and said from now on he would give me a chance to admire him.

He continued to go to her for a few more sessions by himself and I started to refuse to breastfeed Reese in the middle of the night so that I could get my mojo back. I figured if all I had to do was start having more sex and compliment him then we no longer had a problem.

And I was right for another year and a half. We were back to having frequent sex and we never did stop liking each other. We were still madly in love and doing all the things that made each other happy and then I got pregnant again in November 2013. Again, we were full of excitement. We wanted three children to complete our family and we couldn't be more elated with the news.

The pregnancy was going great until 20 weeks in when I started spotting. I went to my obstetrician to see what was causing the spotting and when she checked me I was 1.5 centimeters dilated. She told me I had a 50/50 chance of losing the baby. My heart immediately sank into my stomach. She told me I had to drive myself to the hospital immediately and I would get intravenous medications and lay in bed inverted in an attempt to cause the baby to go back into my womb and stop the labor process.

I agonized over how to tell Jason the news. Finally, after calming myself enough to talk I called him and just said it, "I'm 1.5

centimeters dilated and there is a 50/50 chance that I will lose the baby. I'm on my way to the hospital now."

I began to cry profusely again. I was crushed but told myself that I had to remain positive. 50/50 meant there was a chance that she could be safely delivered and so I had to focus on that 50%.

On the second day in the hospital the doctors told me that if my body could keep the baby in me for three more days then they would sew up my uterus and I would be on bedrest until the baby was born. When Jason heard that he said, "So no sex?!"

I was slightly offended but I understood that for him that was a lifetime. However, for me, I just wanted to do whatever it took to save the baby. I responded with a chuckle, "I knew you would say that. You will be ok. We have to do what's best for the baby."

Two days later our baby girl was born at 21 weeks on March 23, 2014. We named her Heaven. She wasn't strong enough to survive and she passed a little over an hour after her birth. My world stood still and my heart was shattered in a million little pieces.

Jason was my rock. He was such an incredible support. When we said our vows, "...for better or for worse..." I didn't know that this is what our worst was going to be. And I didn't know that I was going to need him in such a way that I did. But he showed up 100%. I saw a side of him that most wives, fortunate for them, never had to see in their husbands. He provided a support system for me that I never knew he had and that I never knew I needed. I felt so close to him in a way that I'd never felt before. My emotional healing process was difficult, to say the least, but having him by my side softened the blow.

I went for my post baby checkup at three weeks. The doctor said I could resume all activity because my body didn't need as much healing time as it did with my other two babies. This was great news because I wanted to start running again. I figured that it would help me get control of my emotions.

I was also given clearance to resume sexual activity but emotionally I wasn't ready. I told Jason that and he said he understood and that he was glad I addressed it with him. He said he was afraid of our marriage falling apart if I couldn't get my sexual desires back. I felt like that was selfish of him to be thinking about sex at a time like this. It had only been three weeks since her birth and I didn't know why that was a concern so early on. I also felt pressured to get myself back together because I didn't want to end up back in counseling.

During my grievance period I started a foundation in Heaven's name and a charity run to help other families who lost their babies prematurely. I was out of work for ten weeks so Jason and I also spent a lot of quality time together. In that time, I was able to peacefully grieve and start to get back to normal. Normal was very different especially outside the house. I felt out of place and uncomfortable but in the comfort of my own home I almost felt whole again. Emotionally I was scarred but all aspects of our marriage and our home life returned to normal.

Heaven's due date was fast approaching in August and I was feeling deep sorrow. I couldn't go for more than three or four weeks without having an emotional breakdown. But now that her due date was right around the corner I was having a hard time getting through each day.

Two weeks before her due date Jason approached me with the taboo topic again. He told me for the third time that he wanted to have sex with other people. I could not believe how insensitive he was being. How could he bring that up or even think about that during such a sensitive time. Amidst my sorrow I was still able to manage having frequent sexual encounters with him. And we didn't have boring sex. We had adventurous, fun and exciting sex so what would possess him to feel this way and more importantly, why now?

In the past I felt sad when he told me these things but this time I was angry. He was being selfish and not considering my emotional state at all. It was like the only thing that mattered was that he was satisfied. Yet, I still felt like I had to get myself together or end up back on someone's couch. I loved frequently frolicking about with him but he was turning what should be fun and effortless, into a somewhat tense situation for me.

For a few weeks Jason went to counseling to try and sort his feelings out. He didn't want to end our marriage and I wasn't really stressing over his desire. My issue was the emotional inconvenience that it caused me every time we had to talk about it. I thought his feelings were normal and that he would never act upon it. What we had was too great to throw away on random sex and I knew that he wasn't 'that guy.'

In the summer of 2015 the topic was touched again and by June 2016 I was starting to have enough. We celebrated ten years of marriage and a month later we celebrated his major accomplishment of earning his doctorate degree. He worked hard for his degree over the last 5 years or so and I was so proud of him. But about three weeks later we were back at square one. This time he said he wanted an open marriage.

"I'm not doing that so we are getting divorced," I calmly said.

I had had enough and just wasn't about to entertain the idea of an open marriage. That was taking it way too far. I was serious about that and he saw the seriousness in my demeanor. I was fed up with him. Not only was he having much more sex than the average married couple, he also had an amazing wife who he called his best friend. I knew my worth and I knew that I was heads and shoulders above the greater majority of wives out there.

He had a dream wife and marriage. He didn't carry a 9 to 5 because he wanted to be free from people telling him what to do and he wanted his own schedule. I stood by him as he started many different business ventures none of which provided a stable source of income. I gave up my idea of being a stay at home mom so that he could pursue his business dreams. I supported him through getting his doctorate, something that he did not plan to use for immediate financial gain but so that he could have a bigger title when he started his own school. He never had to ask permission to hang out with his friends and I never gave him a problem about it. I was very easy to communicate with and other than the issue at hand, we never went to bed angry with each other not one day in 10 years. I was patient and put up with way more than most wives would. So, the way I saw it was, I was doing my part. But what I wasn't going to do was open up my marriage for some other people to join in.

Once again, he said he would go to counseling. This time he picked out the counselor. Her name was Denise and she specialized in unique sex therapy ranging from topics of sex addiction, gender transition, to all things polyamory. I tried so hard to avoid sitting on another couch but in order to save my marriage it was necessary.

Several days after meeting Denise I was driving home from the grocery store when Jason called me. It was pleasantly warm outside and I was riding around with my windows down. He was trying feverishly to convince me to read "More Than Two". It was a book about opening up marriages to include other people. I tried to remain calm but every time he would bring up reading things about open marriages my blood would boil. I didn't need someone else to explain to me why I should allow other people into my marriage. Why I should accept my husband dating and having sex with other women and why I should do the same with men. I couldn't remain calm anymore and my internal switch flipped. I started to get hot and sweat started to bead on my forehead. "You're pissing me off asking me to read some nonsense about why this is ok!" I yelled.

He responded with, "I wish you would just read the book. It's…" I cut him off.

With the loudest voice that I could pull from inside me I shouted, "I'm not reading shit!"

My head was shaking as I stuck my neck out and ever so ignorantly enunciated "shit." By now my armpits were sweating and I was feeling slightly faint. I rolled the windows up and blasted the air conditioner to cool off. 'Fuck it!' I hung up.

As soon as the call was disconnected I dialed up my good friend Stephanie, the only other person that knew about this part of my marriage other than Eric and Kris. A sweet southern voice picked up the line, "Hey."

By now the saliva in my mouth had turned thick and white. As soon as I opened my mouth it started flying everywhere. "Yo! This motherfucker keeps talking 'bout me reading some book. I'm not reading no motherfucking book about why I should let him fuck some other chicks. He must be outta his motherfucking mind!"

I commenced to shout and curse and spit for the next five minutes as I drove home. It seemed like with every new thought my foot would step on the gas pedal jolting the car forward. I managed to arrive home safely. I parked the car in the garage, closed the garage door and rolled the windows down. I was still shouting but the words echoed off the garage walls and started to hurt my own ears. Finally, I got silent. I had nothing left to say and I started to silently cry. Stephanie still had not said a word since she answered the phone and said hello. I was taking deep breaths because I didn't want her to know I was crying. Then, I punched the steering wheel letting the last of my anger out.

"Do you want me to come over?" Stephanie asked ever so gently.

"No. I don't want him to know that I have told you. Can I come over there?"

"Of course, you can. You can spend the night and we can eat the cupcakes." She said excitedly.

A big grin covered my face. Stephanie bought two cannabis cupcakes that we decided to save for the perfect time and what could be more perfect then now.

I got off the phone, packed an overnight bag, and jumped in the shower. I stopped by the grocery store to pick up food for our munchies. I had never consumed cannabis of any sort before so I was super siked and nervous. The conversation with Jason was fading in my mind and I was just thinking about the fun that I was about to have. I loved hanging with Stephanie because we always had a great time together. She knew how to make me laugh and understood what I was going through. She'd been divorced for several years.

When I arrived at her home the aroma of bacon filled my senses. I'd given up eating meat about half a year ago but every once in a while, I would turn back to bacon and sausage. Just the smell of it made me happy. Stephanie had just put the French toast casserole and sausage in the oven and started to peel and season the shrimp. We also had cheese Doritos and gummy bears (only the red and green ones) to help us with our munchies.

We were eating, cooking and laughing. Once everything was prepared we sat all of the food on the kitchen island and we laughed a good hearty laugh. "Look at all of this food!" I exclaimed.

We laughed some more at how greedy we were being. But food was one of the things that made our friendship so great. "Are you sure we need this much food?"

"Yes! When you're high you want to chew," she explained with a chuckle.

I don't know why I questioned her. What did it matter? I just liked eating.

After satisfying our stomachs I said, "Ok. Are you ready?"

She took two cupcakes out of the refrigerator. One for both of us. We marveled over the beauty of the design. I think we were both sort of nervous because it never took us that long to bite into anything no matter how good it looked. Many comments passed by and we both took a fork, picked a piece off and stuck it in our mouths at the same time. "Yuck! This tastes like soap!" I exclaimed.

She didn't really like hers either but we ate them nonetheless. About half way through I said, "I don't feel anything."

"Me either," she responded.

So, we switched cupcakes and proceeded to finish them off. Even the crumbs. Then the giggles started. We were talking about who knows what and then she put her hand over her face and rubbed her eyes, "Oh my God... you just... my goodness... I'm still confused damn it."

I didn't know what she was talking about and I was laughing uncontrollably. I could hardly catch my breath. Then she started to do the choo choo train towards the other end of the room. "Choo-choo," she said as she motioned being a choo-choo train.

I could hardly breath I was laughing so much. Then the choo-choo train turned into the James Brown dance. I was so happy amidst the chaos that happened earlier.

We laughed and laughed and laughed some more and then I started to feel pins and needles at the back of my neck. My entire body felt flushed with warmth and the pins and needles started to spread to my head. "Damn it! I don't want to be high anymore!" I said panicking.

I went from laughter to shear panic in a matter of seconds. Stephanie had more control over herself and told me to have a seat. I couldn't sit and I asked her, "If I drink a lot of water do you think I'll stop being high?"

"I don't think so. Just sit the fuck down and relax," she ordered feeling my panic.

I sat down and the pins and needles faded. "Take my picture," I said.

I was no longer scared and the giggles had returned. I tried to pose but couldn't stop laughing long enough for her to take a picture. I put my hands on my waist and sat up real straight. "How about this? Do I look high?" I asked through waves of laughter.

"Yo! I'm high!" I said as I continued to laugh out of control.

Then I panicked again and started pacing the floor shouting, "Abort! Abort!"

By now Stephanie was sitting on the couch just looking at me. "Sit down," she said.

She turned the television on and we both tried to focus on the show to control our high. I just wanted to go to sleep because I couldn't stand the feeling. I laid my head back on the couch and tried to close my eyes but I kept getting paranoid and opening my eyes real wide. I told myself to just relax and it will pass.

Then Stephanie got up holding her stomach. Next thing I knew she was vomiting everywhere. It was all over the kitchen wall, the carpet and the countertop. I just sat there helplessly looking at her. "I wish I could help you but I can't move," I managed to say.

I repeated that several times and then asked, "Are you ok?"

"I'm ok," she answered.

She managed to get herself to the bathroom where she stayed for longer then I was awake. It seemed like time was standing still but the television kept playing so I figured life had not stopped around me. I tried to stay awake until she came out of the bathroom but eventually I drifted to sleep.

The next morning I could hardly move. I was extremely dizzy and it hurt just to turn my head to the side. I laughed to myself as I thought about the foolishness that we'd gotten ourselves into. I felt like I was going to die the night before but it beat what I had waiting for me at home.

After about two weeks of Jason and I going to counseling together we were finally able to move forward in our marriage. For the next year we continued to enjoy each other as he continued to see Denise on and off when he started to feel the desire to have sex with other women. Even though we were still in deep like with each other, I started to fear for our marriage. I started to realize that he wasn't letting this idea of other women go and about half a year later I said to Stephanie, "I think ultimately we are going to end in divorce."

She was shocked to hear me say that and responded, "Why?"

"Because he typically sticks with how he feels. Every year this gets worse and it's gonna get to a point that it can't be fixed anymore," I answered.

"You don't want to be divorced," she said passionately.

She had three children ranging in ages from six to twelve when she got divorced.

"Yes I do. If this is what he wants then that's what's going to happen," I said.

Little did I know, I was about to experience exactly what she said that I didn't want, almost eight weeks after celebrating our 11th anniversary.

Chapter 4

Tipping Point

"Are you awake?" asked an excited Jason.

Behind my eyelids I could tell it was still dark. I squinted my eyes open to confirm. Then, I turned my head to the left where an excited Jason was on his knees, arms stretched across the bed with a huge grin plastered across his face. I answered curiously, "I am now."

"Get packed! We're going on an adventure!" Jason said full of energy.

I instantly sat straight up in the bed and let out an excited, "We are! Where are we going? Are you serious?" My cheeks were hurting from smiling so hard.

"Wear something athletic and pack something athletic and two chill outfits," he cheerfully said. I could feel his excitement from across the bed. He probably had not slept all night waiting for the 5:30 hour to wake me up.

I still didn't move because my body was tired but my brain was ready for an adventure. "What! Are you serious?" I repeated several times.

"Get out the bed and pack," he playfully ordered.

"Ok. Ok. Oh snap! We're going on an adventure!" I finally got out of the bed to pack. I was in a daze and couldn't wait to see what Jason had in store for my 40th birthday.

After dropping Joi and Reese off to school we headed towards my surprise. "I'm so excited but so sleepy. Can I go back to sleep?" I asked.

"Yup! Sleep now," he answered.

That made me wonder. Sleep now? What adventure laid ahead of me? I closed my eyes and drifted back to sleep.

An hour later I was awakened. "Babe! We're here!" Jason announced.

My lips started to curve into a huge smile as my eyes opened and in front of me was beautiful green shrubbery that was surrounded by an immaculately manicured lawn. The shrubbery was the background for the large white sign 'Callaway Gardens.' We were at a resort that had gigantic beautiful trees and brightly colored flower bushes everywhere I looked. It was like we had drove into nature's paradise. I rolled the windows down so that I could hear the birds chirping. The smell of early morning dew rushed into the car and I took a deep breath to soak in the entire experience.

"Callaway! How beautiful! You're the best! I'm so excited!" I leaned over to him and he turned his face towards me and I planted a big kiss on his lips.

After checking in we decided to roam the grounds and see what we could get into. Jason knew that I loved being outdoors amongst nature and physical challenges. So, our first activity was bike riding. The bikes had super wide handlebars with large thin tires that had the feel of the '70's. We put our snacks in the basket that hung on the handle bars and started our adventure together.

The bike path was lined with enormous trees that seemed to dance together as we rode by them. At their roots were beautiful flowers and shrubs that made a breathtaking scenery. "Jason, this is just perfect! It's so beautiful and quite out here. This is the perfect way to start 40. Thank you!"

He responded saying, "I knew you would love it."

He was beaming with pride. He wanted to create something memorable and he did just that in the first hour of our adventure.

As we rode up and coasted down the rolling hills we marveled at the aesthetically pleasing scenery. Then the path started to border a huge lake. "Want to go canoeing?" Jason asked.

"Sure!" I responded full of excitement.

We put our bikes down and headed towards the boats. "Be careful when you get in. Many people have tipped over before they even get out of the dock," the instructor said.

Jason was very careful stepping in and made sure I was equally careful for he feared the life living below the waters. He sat at the tail end of the canoe and stretched his legs forward. The instructor handed us our paddles, gave us a few useful tips and we headed out to explore the waters.

After we left the dock we had a good laugh because we had difficulty coordinating our strokes and we were going in circles trying to move forward. After some trial and error we finally figured out how to propel forward.

It was so quiet on the water. All we could hear was the rocking of the waves. The sky had scattered chunky white clouds amidst a light blue background. The skyline was interrupted by enormous trees making the view even more serene. We didn't talk much. We just shared our appreciation for the moment that we were in.

After returning the canoe to its dock we were famished. We hopped back onto our bikes to return them so we could sit down for a good meal.

Jason had everything planned out. He took me to a delectable seafood restaurant because he knew that anytime there was seafood involved, I was happy.

Later that evening we sat outside in the common grounds at our hotel. We were enjoying each other's company with good conversation and drinks and then he said, "I want to go to the playboy mansion one day."

"Huh. That could be interesting," I said.

He went on to talk about the things that we could do in the mansion. I was always up for having sex in public places. I would say to him, "If no one tells us that they saw us then what's the harm?"

I usually had to get him to warm up to the idea but once he was warm, it was like being behind closed doors. So, I thought he was moving in a different direction, one that I usually had to start.

"So we can do it one day?" He asked excited.

"Yeah. That can happen one day," I responded.

With a huge grin he said, "That's something to really look forward to. It's on my bucket list."

I started to wonder if maybe I heard something different. Maybe I answered yes to the wrong question and so I inquired, "Wait. What did you ask me?"

"If we could switch partners when we go to the mansion or have a threesome," he responded.

My guard went up. Here we go again. On my birthday? I calmly and sternly said, "No. I'm not doing that. I thought you just said we would go to the mansion and have sex there or something."

"You know that's something that I desire," he stated.

"Nah. I'm not doing that. I'll go to the mansion but I'm not doing that," I made myself clear.

The mood was ruined and I started another topic of conversation.

The next morning we went out to a local restaurant for breakfast. He told me that we were going zip lining afterwards and that we needed to hurry up before we missed our time slot. So when he drove up to the location for zip lining I hopped out the car before he could even turn the ignition off. "Wait for me!" He yelled.

I kept on running almost at full speed towards the building as I yelled, "I don't want to miss our spot!"

When I arrived at the check-in window there was one person ahead of me. I was slightly irritated because they weren't moving fast enough. Then I felt a tap on my shoulder. A strange annoyance came over me because I couldn't imagine why anyone would be taping me. After all, I was next in line. So, I turned around with a look of serious business on my face. "Dave!!!" I exclaimed.

Dave was our friend from home. He didn't say anything he just smiled and gave me a big hug. "What are you doing here?" I asked with great surprise.

And then his wife, my good friend of nine years, said, "Surprise!"

"What are you doing here?" I said as I hugged her.

As I was hugging her I saw Jason jogging up to us with an enormous grin. "Oh my goodness!" I exclaimed.

I had no other words. I was in total shock. After the excitement came down I realized that there was no real rush so we talked and casually got registered.

"I'm gonna go to the bathroom," I announced as I walked backwards away from the registration booth.

As I backed away I noticed someone slowly peak out from the left side of the building. I threw my hands up over my head in total and utter shock. I just stared with a smile that made my face ache. Then I bent over and shook my head. My eyes started to swell with tears and I could tell that if I spoke they would know that I was choked up. I stood up quickly so the tears wouldn't fall and I put my arms over my head again. I said nothing. I just stood there gazing at Kris. She was beaming just as much as I was. She wore a blue running shirt and black Capri spandex which told me she would be joining in on the fun. I only saw her about once, maybe twice a year and she looked exactly as I'd last seen her. She stood maybe an inch or two shorter than me with golden light brown skin. She had a jolly smile that lit up her super cute face. Her hair was long and flowing perfectly and she looked as though she had been hitting the gym.

Finally, we walked towards each other and I said the only thing that wouldn't produce a bucket of tears, "Oh my goodness."

We shared a long warm embrace. Kris had flown there form New Jersey just to celebrate me. My heart was touched tremendously.

"Well, who else is coming?" I asked playfully as I started to look around for more people.

"I don't know," Jason said just as playfully as he gave me a hug and kissed my cheek.

I let out a long, "Aaahhh! You got me!"

I finally went to the bathroom and when I returned there were two more. Rennie and Sasha, Rennie's fiancé, had joined the crew. I was so excited to have my brother and friends join me as I entered a new decade.

After zip lining we sat down to eat lunch together and then said our goodbyes. I thanked everyone for coming out to hang with me and they all parted except for Kris. She was staying the night with us. We walked around the grounds together and then she and Jason decided they wanted to take a look at the cottages.

After arriving and getting out of the cars, Jason and Kris walked a few steps behind me. As I approached the front door Jason said, "They're having an open house so the door should be open."

When I opened the door I could see silver and gold balloons and food set up on the kitchen island. I was instantly happy because I was starving. In the very next moment a clamor of voices were heard from inside, "Surprise!"

I stumbled, catching myself from falling as my arms reached for the wall behind me. "What!" I shouted.

All of the guests from earlier were still there plus two more! Again I stood in utter disbelief. "Oh my goodness!" was all I could manage to say, accentuating each word with that same smile from earlier in the day.

Then I hugged my two new guests, thanked everyone again for being there and gave Jason another huge hug and kiss.

I looked around and admired the decorations. On the kitchen island sat a variety of foods; fried fish and oysters, French fries, a vegetable medley, and tarter sauce for baked shrimp. There was a small, fancy, gold lined chalkboard with 'Vanessa' written on it and cute little doodles around it sitting amongst the food.

The dining table was long and probably sat eight to ten people. It had a white tablecloth and gold lettering on it that spelled out happy birthday. The table was full of goodies. There was a chocolate cake with the number 40 sticking out of it, a variety of cupcakes with different types of frosting and colorful swirls for icing, three fancy glass jars that had powdered donuts in one and two different types of gourmet popcorn in the other two. There were gold balloons in the shape of 40 laying on the table and gold and white utensils and such.

"Do you like it?" Jason asked.

"I love it!' I exclaimed.

Then he said, "Great! Look around. There are four bedrooms and four bathrooms and we are all staying here tonight!"

"What! We're having a party and everyone is staying the night here?" I said, about to burst with joy.

"Yup!" he responded with such pride.

I hugged him tight and laid my head against his chest. I closed my eyes and said thank you. Shakiness could be heard in my voice and I turned my head away from them before a tear dropped. "Awww. Are you crying?" asked Sasha.

"No," I lied. My heart was so full.

We ate and laughed and sang happy birthday and then one of my all-time favorite songs came on by the Notorious B.I.G. I knew all the words to "Get Money" and after having a few libations I was ready to party. Jason recited B.I.G.'s lyrics and then I looked at him, started swaying from side to side and started to recite Little Kim's verse. I got close to him and waved my hand in his face as I flowed to the vibe of the music.

Then the old school rap song 'Jump' came on by Kris Kross. He and I stood side by side and recited the entire song as we jumped to every command to "jump jump". Our guests laughed and jumped with us. I had a blast that night.

We all entertained each other until 2 in the morning and then Jason and I had our own form of entertainment behind closed doors.

The next morning we woke up and had mimosas, fruit and bagels on the patio. I felt so loved. Jason had gone all out and I couldn't wait to conjure up how to celebrate his 40th in two years.

One of Jason's dreams was to start a school. He was finally pursing that dream and the school was ready to be opened. It just needed students. He and his business partner, Tina, had their first open house six weeks after my birthday. I eagerly helped out at the event because I was so proud of him for finally making it happen. Two days later the ground fell from beneath me.

We were in the kitchen chatting about the day's events when he leaned up against the stove and folded his arms. That grin that he always had when he had something uncomfortable to say was on his face as he said, "I need to talk to you about something that's been burning a hole in my pocket. But first I want to give you a hug and I want you to know how much I love you," he said.

Here we go again I thought as I stood up from the bottom stair I was sitting on. We embraced as my heart started to pound in anticipation of another of Jason's revelations.

...garble, garble, garble.... "I can't be monogamous anymore," he said.

Followed by my calmness, "Then we are getting divorced."

Jason proceeded to run down the reasons that he can't be monogamous and how polygamy could be great for our marriage. He said that he'd been researching polyamory and he feels that he is polyamorous. According to him, polyamorous people have intimate relationships with more than one partner, with the knowledge of all partners involved and they are capable of loving more than one person. He told me how it can be practiced ethically and responsibly and that it would make us even more trusting of each other. "Once we get past the jealousy we will become even closer," he said.

We exchanged opposing opinions for an hour. We both remained calm but by the end I snapped. I came out of my relaxed position on the stairs with my foot raised against the wall. I sat straight up, feet planted firmly on the ground and started to yell obscenities.

"We can't even have a fucking conversation without you getting outta control!" he yelled.

Did he just scorn me because I won't allow polygamy in my marriage?

Then he postured up and said, "Vanessa, if you're going to divorce me anyway, why don't you just see what it feels like first? See what it feels like for me to come home after a date."

I spewed out, "Are you fucking crazy! Have you lost your fucking mind!?"

He then resorted to asking me to read the book 'More than Two' again. "It's about people like me," he said.

He asked if I'd read it over the next two weeks or so and then we could go to counseling.

"I'm not reading shit!" I screamed.

My blood was boiling and I couldn't stop cursing and mumbling, my head twisted with every thought "....you want me to read some shit about people like you.....you musta lost your fucking mind....and what the fuck am I gonna do while you're on these dates....huh....you must be fucking crazy....," I said spitting fire.

As I headed upstairs to the bedroom he said, "I'll sleep in the playroom."

"Yeah. You damn right," I said to myself.

The next morning I called out of work. I hated lying but I couldn't possibly tell Lisa, my friend and boss, what went on the night before. I told her some story about my mother being sick. Then I called Mimi to tell her what was going on. She knew what happened last year so I just had to catch her up to last night's fiasco.

Then I called Kris. A pleasant, "Hello," answered the phone.

Through my tears I managed to say, "I'm not doing this anymore."

A concerned voice spoke back, "Why are you crying? What happened?"

I told her everything. It was nothing she had not heard before but this time I was done.

"Well where are you going?" she asked.

"I'm going to the park to listen to this ridiculous ass book," I answered.

After hanging up with her I pulled over to the shoulder on the interstate. I downloaded the book 'More Than Two' and tapped play. My thought, let me read this shit so we can move on.

When I arrived at the park I packed some snacks and water in my pockets. The trees were so tall and formed a welcoming walkway into nature. I proceeded to walk through the shaded pathway. It was only in the 8 o'clock hour so the June air felt light and cool on my arms.

As I walked and listened to the book, I learned about all kinds of shit. Why people need open relationships, how to open a relationship, how to manage jealousy, how children are impacted.

I walked for miles and hours. After about 2 hours I was ready to head back to my car and that's when I realized I was lost. "Well how am I supposed to get outta here?" I mumbled out loud.

I turned on my GPS and was walked right into a dead end. My feet were hurting and I needed to take a seat. I walked toward what I thought was the right direction and rested in front of a rather murky lake. The grass was misty but I didn't care. I sat down, planted my feet and hugged my knees as I learned more about different ways to make an open marriage work.

I sat there for about an hour while I ate my snacks and then I needed to get some more fuel in my body. I gathered myself together and walked towards my car so that I could go somewhere to eat lunch.

By now, I was listening to the book at 1.5 times speed. My mind had been subdued to this nonsense for about 4 hours. Damn! How much longer will it take to finish this book I thought?

I ate lunch and then drove to another park so I could sit some more. I walked until I found the perfect bench. I sat my water down, stretched out and sped up the book to 1.75 times. All the while experiencing waves of anger.

After several hours passed I was able to adjust my ears to double time and finished the book in 8 hours. This is the shit he wants to do? "Oh hell no," I thought.

And so I called him to bash this bullshit that I subjected myself to over the last 8 hours. "Hello," he answered.

"I listened to the whole book and I'm not doing that shit!" I yelled.

"Can I call you back in a few minutes? I just stepped out of a meeting about the school to answer your call."

What the fuck?! Click! Why the fuck did he answer the phone if he couldn't talk?

I was boiling waiting for the phone to ring again. Several minutes later Jason's name ran across my phone screen and I answered yelling, "I listened to it and if that's what you want then we are done!"

"I started to listen to some of it today and that's not really what...." he started to say as I cut him off.

"You had me listen to this entire book and that's not what you want? Well let me tell you what else happened in the book!" I shouted.

My hands flew in the air and my body was slightly distorted as my head shook from side to side while I told him all of the bullshit that I read. I couldn't decide if I wanted to stand or sit as spit flew out of my mouth while I ran down all the shit that I wasn't going to do.

And at the end I shouted loud enough for the entire park to here, "I'm divorcing you! From here on out we are separated! I don't have time right now but I will file the papers as soon as the run is over! I'm not your wife anymore! And my name is Vanessa! Not Babe! Don't call or text me for nothing if it doesn't involve the kids! You don't have a wife anymore!"

BANG! Conversation was over and I hung the phone up.

And I immediately sent a follow up text, 'I FUCKING HATE YOU!!!!!!!!!!!'

Exhaustion was all over me as I drove home and fear started to take over. My babies were awaiting my arrival while Mimi entertained them. I was afraid the weariness of the day would show. Afraid my eyes would start to weep the moment I looked at them. My heart was racing. Calm. Calm. Calm. You can do this. You got this. It's ok I told myself.

No! This shit wasn't ok. And I don't got this! Anxiety started to creep up on me. I can't do it. I can't face my babies. I can't let them see me like this. Panic started to take over. Stop! Mimi can help I thought. So I called her. She answered so soft and calm. Lovingly.

My voice was shaking. "I'm on my way home but can you please stay. I'm trying to get myself together but..." Silence. And then the tears that I was trying so desperately to hold fell.

"I'll stay. Whatever you need," she said

The tears started flowing again but I managed a, "Thank you," to exit my lips.

"I love you," she told me.

Mimi ended all of her phone calls with I love you but I knew this one was different. This one came from deep down in her gut. She loved me and felt helpless that she couldn't help me and her son who was the root of the pain.

I drove the car to the nearest parking lot and pulled the sun visor down and flipped open the mirror. I had to wipe away all evidence of tears and sorrow. I had to stand strong in the face of my children.

As I approached the house I saw Joi playing with her friends outside. They were running around, joyous screams of playful fun echoed through the air. Joi came running when she spotted the car shouting, "Mommy!"

I mustered up a half smile. "Hey baby," I said as I opened the door and wrapped my arms around her so tight.

"Where's Reese?" I asked.

She shook her shoulders up, tilted her head to the side and answered, "He's taking a nap."

And then she ran off to join in with her friends.

When I entered the house I immediately smelled the aroma of what Mimi was preparing for dinner. My senses told me it was spaghetti that was filling the air. Jason and the children loved spaghetti. Fuck Jason! Who cares what he loves! Calm Vanessa. Calm.

I embraced Mimi. No need to hide from her. She didn't ask the routine question of how was your day. She just looked into my face. I felt like I should speak but say what. My face told it all. So I slowly shook my head back and forth, curled my lips and shrugged my shoulders and said "Thank you."

"Where is Reese?" I asked.

She pointed to the couch as if to whisper, "quite."

The best part of my day layed on the couch peacefully in a bright orange shirt with tan shorts. I picked him up and laid him on my chest. He smelled of the outdoors. The aroma of a dirty little boy in the June heat took over my nose but I didn't care. I propped a couch pillow under my head and closed my eyes. I hugged him so tight yet gentle for fear of waking him. I kissed the top of his head repeatedly.

As worn out as I was, I didn't want to fall asleep. I just wanted to feel him in my arms. I started to relive when he was an itty bitty baby. Jason and I would sit on this same couch and watch TV late at night. We would take turns holding him on our chest while he slept. And then my brain became flooded with the conversation from the night before. I started to envision my new future without Jason. I envisioned raising my children as a single mom.

My chest started to rise and fall quickly. My breathing became heavier. My eyes began to water as my palms became moist. My lips started to frown and I couldn't stop them. Think happy thoughts. Think happy thoughts.

And then Joi came ramming through the door. My face quickly straightened up but my eyes were still full of tears. "Shhhh!" I whispered as I put my finger over my mouth and closed my eyes.

Damn it! Closing my eyes made the tears trickle out. And then Reese woke up. "Hey son," I said.

He didn't respond. He just tried to squirm out of the firm hold I had on him. We playfully rustled for a few seconds and then I let him go. "Hello!" I said as I caught his arm.

"Hi," he responded and running off he went.

"Why do you have tears in your eyes Mommy?" Joi inquisitively asked.

"I was yawning and rubbing them. That makes them tear," I confidently responded.

She shrugged and said, "Ok," as she took off running.

I decided I'd join them outside. I wiped the tears from my eyes and I grabbed my comfy stadium seat from the garage. I sat it at the edge of the driveway as I felt the sun beam on my face. I gazed into the sky, away from the sun, and admired the perfectly blue sky and fluffy appearing white clouds.

Damn! This is my new life I thought. Just me and my babies. A tsunami had rocked our family and they had no clue. They were living the life of Riley...you know... not a care in the world. I didn't know how this was going to play out but here's what I knew for sure, my babies weren't going to suffer because of their selfish ass father. And I will make it through this. I didn't know how but I knew I would.

"Moooommmyyyy!!!" Reese shouted as he plowed into my knees with his arms stretched out wide.

He wrapped them around my waist and laid his head in my lap. I rubbed his back and kissed the top of his head and managed to mustered up a, "Are you having fun?"

"No!" he exclaimed.

I chuckled and shook my head. He never admitted to enjoying himself. I watched him running and screaming sounds of delight, playing tag and riding his scooter but he wasn't having fun. "Well you looked like you were having fun," I said.

"I wasn't," he insisted.

"Ok," I said letting go of the issue.

He climbed into my lap and swung his legs vigorously and then jumped off as if he were jumping off a ledge. And then he took off in a zigzag motion running with all his might to catch up with his sister and the neighborhood kids.

I took a deep breath and exhaled. I couldn't believe that we had reached this point. What we had was so perfect that I just couldn't understand why that wasn't enough. I couldn't understand why he would want to introduce other women into our union. He not only wanted to have sex with these women but he also wanted to share his life with them and they share their life with him. For me, the thought of him sharing his dreams, his daily ups and downs and his spirit with other women was too much for me to handle. It was too hurtful.

I saw him changing over the past five years or so. He was evolving into a free spirit that wanted to buck all systems, even the bond that we formed and the oath that we took. He was no longer the man that I knew. I could not allow that lifestyle in my marriage so as much as I didn't want my children to hurt, I couldn't see polygamy in my marriage either.

Later that evening Joi and Reese lay in their beds peacefully. Reese can't sleep in a dark room by himself. His room is always brightly lit. I don't know how he can fall asleep with the light shining on his eyeballs like that. But he would always insist on having it on. I turned the room light off and pulled the baseball on the lamp. That light wasn't so bright.

I kneeled at Reese's side. The floor was taking a toll on my 40-year-old knees. I stared at him as I often did after Heaven was born. She looked so much like him. He was a shade of light brown with a cute button nose. He had full pink lips with a dimple in his chin. He also had dimples in his cheeks when he smiled. His hair was dark brown and curly. I often wondered where he got his curly hair from until I cut mine about an inch from my scalp. We had the same curly hair that made people say, "Oh you two have that good hair."

He was a cute kid, a smaller version of Jason. I prayed that Reese didn't turn into his father one day. I prayed that I can instill in him the importance of keeping a family together. My sight became blurry. The tears were starting again.

"Please don't be like your father." I whispered.

"Please... Please...Please...Please..." I had to stop myself. I stared some more.

"I love you so much son," I whispered.

I kissed him on his soft cheek, his forehead, right behind his ear. Then I placed my hand on his head and caressed his cheek.

I stood up and headed towards Joi's room. Between their rooms stood the bathroom. I usually looked into the bathroom to make sure she had cleaned it. I was usually so aggravated because of its mess and I would want to wake her out her sleep to clean it. I never did though.

Anyway, on that night I didn't look in there because I didn't want to be aggravated with what didn't even matter. Her room was dark. I covered up her foot that was sticking out of the covers. I kneeled on my old knees again. I rubbed her back and stared at her. "She's going to be so hurt," I thought to myself.

"I'm sorry Joi," I whispered.

She always loved family time. This was going to crush her. How could he leave this? How the fuck could he leave this? He's going to break her heart. I shook my head back and forth as if in brand new amazement and I repeated many times, "Wow!" Each time getting a little louder.

Anger and rage washed over me as I stared at Joi. Then I kissed her several times on the cheek and forehead as I rubbed her back. My babies....

I ran the shower water and before I stepped into the shower I looked myself in the eyes through the mirror. I saw sorrow and grief. My eyes looked tired. My face solemn. I couldn't even muster up a smile. What was there to smile about?

I stood in the shower for what seemed like an eternity as the warm water ran down my back. I stood lifeless and thought about all of the amazing times that Jason and I shared. And then anger creeped in again. Is this really it? I'm tripping! I'm going to be divorced? I'm going to be a single mother because of some unknown women?

I leaned forward and rested my forehead on the shower wall. My hands were placed on the wall, slightly above my head. I could smell the soap that I had not picked up yet. My mind and body were weak. I began to sob. The sobbing turned into gut wrenching crying and I could not stand on my feet any longer. I fell to my knees, my head hung low. I pleaded with God to turn this around.

"Help me! Please! Help me! Please! Help me! Jesus! Help me! I can't lose my husband. Please help me. Tell me what to do."

What started out as an angry cry to God became a quite defeated plea. I stopped crying and just sat there on my knees. And then my heart began to race. My breathing became heavy. I started to feel hot. A wave of panic came over me and wouldn't leave.

I felt like I needed to get out! I needed to run! I didn't know what was happening to me. Was I dying? I wanted to scream out "HELP ME," but I couldn't because I didn't want to scare the children. Did I need medical attention? What the fuck was going on?

I stood up in a crazy panic and thrust the shower door open. The cool air rushed in as the warm shower water continued to beat on me. I felt my heart rate slow down. My breathing wasn't so quick. Panic started to leave me. From inside the shower I looked around the bathroom. I was scared. Just seeing the bathroom as it should be provided a strange relief for me.

I reached up and grabbed my wash cloth that was hanging on the top of the shower stall. I rubbed the soap between the wash cloth and my hands. Soap was hitting the bathroom floor. My body was cold and I began to shiver. Puddles were forming on the floor. I wanted to close the door but I was afraid. I washed my body quickly, trying my best not to make too much of a mess.

After drying off I stood limp in front of the mirror. I looked pathetic. I needed to take my ass to bed. I hoped Jason didn't come home that night.

First order of business the next day was calling Denise. She'd been Jason's therapist for the past year. He said he felt safe with her because she would not judge him. I didn't care who he saw, as long as he was talking to someone about his problem.

I drove to a nearby park to make the phone call. My heart began to race as I looked up her number in my phone. "Hello. This is Denise," she answered.

A lump was in my throat. I paused and gathered my thoughts but I couldn't stop the tears. "Ummm....hi. This is Vanessa Love."

"Hello Vanessa," she responded with concern in her voice.

"Can I come see you? Ummm...Jason said he can't be monogamous anymore and so I told him we are getting divorced." By now my chest was heaving, I could no longer see in front of me and I was completely vulnerable. Forty-eight hours had not even passed yet and I felt like I had totally lost the fight. I was physically weak. I felt like I had no fight left.

"I can tell you are in a bad place. Are you able to come in today?" she asked.

Of course, I had time and two hours later I arrived at her office. She looked exactly as I remembered her from last year. She stood about 5 feet 5 inches tall. Her hair was brunette and shoulder length. She had perfectly clear cream-colored skin that made her look like a healthy 50 year old women. Her eyes were dark brown and always showed concerned. When I first met her I immediately got the vibe that she was trustworthy. Today she wore a light blue buttoned-down shirt and a dark blue blazer with a blue and white striped tie, tan khakis and navy blue loafers. She greeted me with a hug that said, 'this is business but I feel your pain.'

Jason was in her office only two months back so I caught her up to speed. By now I had two panic attacks in the last twelve hours. She told me how to manage them and asked if I was willing to take something to relieve the attacks. I told her that I started taking anti-anxiety herbs the day before and I was just waiting for them to start working.

After giving her more insight she asked if I wanted to have a session with him tomorrow. I almost felt like I'd hit the lottery. "Yes!" I responded anxiously with a smile.

I was starting to feel better about everything. I texted him to see if that would be ok. He agreed.

Another sleepless night passed. Jason slept on the couch and I layed in the bed all night as my thoughts rambunctiously ran through my head. I kept telling myself to go to sleep and think about it in the morning but that's so much easier said than done. My alarm sounded at six a.m. I drug myself out of bed and got dressed as if I were going to work. I didn't want my children to ask me why I had so much time off and what I was doing all day so I just pretended to go to work every day. Jason was already out of the house before I was dressed.

"Good morning," I greeted Mimi before I left for the day.

She was going to watch Joi and Reese. There was nothing actually good about the morning but it was the polite thing to say.

"How are you this morning?" She asked in a very concerned voice as she gave me a hug.

"Terrible," I answered in a completely deflated voice.

She gently shook her head up and down and said, "I understand."

Joi and Reese lay comfortably asleep. I kissed them on the cheek and left the house for the day. I was going to spend the morning in the park until it was time to head out to see Denise. I was hopeful.

I took with me an old comforter so that I could lay out at the park if I wanted to. I was so exhausted that 30 minutes after waking up I was already ready for a nap. Once at the park I sat in the car for a bit as I talked to Kris. I shared many things with her and she listened intently. She knew Jason very well and gave me some good things to think about while going through this process. She assured me that Jason loved me and that I would be ok with whatever happened. I believed both of those things but I just didn't know how and when I would get to the part about being ok because at that moment I was so broken.

After that conversation I decided to get out and take a walk around the park. I had gospel playing in my earphones as I tried to clear my spirit of negativity. As I was walking I felt the panic rise again. I started to get nervous because I began to be afraid that I would not be able to talk myself out of the attack. I turned the music up to try to fight it. I started taking deep breaths and walking faster, swinging my arms fiercely as if preparing for a fight. My stride became longer and I wanted to run away but knew that the attack would not disappear if I did. I began to sing the words of Yolanda Adams, 'The Battle is the Lord's out loud. I shouted as I threw my arms up to the sky, "...hold your head up high, don't you cry it's the Lord's…"

My heart was racing and I could barely breathe. I was gasping for air as I belted out, "...no matter what it is that you're going through, hold your head up, stick your chest out, and remember he's using you, for this battle is not yours alone, this battle is not yours, you cannot and you will not do it all by yourself, this battle is not yours, the lord is the only one who can fight it..."

I was singing as if my life depended on it and at that moment I felt like it did. I was not only afraid of the attacks but I was also afraid that one day I may not be able to sing it away or talk myself down from it. So, I sang loud and forceful as if I was pushing it out of my body. And when the song ended I leaned over and put my hands on my knees. I was having trouble breathing and the heaving from crying was making it difficult to compose myself.

I replayed the song as I continued to lean on my knees. I sang calmly the parts that I could as I tried to catch my breath. When I finally stood back up there were two older ladies walking past me. I could tell that they had been watching all along. I wondered what they were thinking but didn't care much about the answer. They looked like praying women so I hoped that they would take that moment and pray for me.

The panic attack totally wiped me out and I still had one and a half hours to go until my counseling session with Jason. I went to the car and got my comforter. I spread it out on a concrete slab under a tree. I layed on it not caring about who was around or how hard the concrete was on my backside. I looked up at the

77

heavens and silently prayed. I turned the music off because I just needed silence. Eventually my eyes got heavy enough to close and I drifted off to sleep.

When I woke up it was time to head to Denise's office. I felt crazy. A feeling that I was getting too familiar with. I'd gone through three intense emotions in just five hours. Now I was trying to break my current spirit of hatred, the fourth emotion, and develop a spirit of openness. I knew that in order to get anywhere with Jason I would have to be willing to listen, express myself in a way that I could be heard and watch the volume of my voice.

I arrived about 20 minutes early. I sang the words to Whitney Houston's "I Didn't Know My Own Strength". I looked myself in the eyes through the visor and sang the words,"...I thought I'd never make it through, I had no hope to hold on to, I thought I would break, I didn't know my own strength, and I crashed down and I tumbled but I did not crumble. I got through all of the pain. I didn't know my own strength. Survived my darkest hour, my faith kept me alive. I picked myself back up, held my head up high, I was not built to break. I didn't know my own strength...there were so many times I wondered how I'd get through the night I thought I took all I could take. I didn't know my own strength..."

Tears were flowing down my face and I didn't care about any bystanders. I was living those words and I knew with everything inside of me that I would make it through this, with or without Jason. I couldn't see the end, but I knew that somehow, I would survive.

My own private therapy session was over and it was time to face Jason. I walked into the building with my eyes darted at the floor. I didn't want to make eye contact with anyone and if he was already there I didn't want to see him without Denise. We managed to avoid each other since the evening that he shattered my world.

I took a seat in the waiting room. He wasn't there yet. "I Didn't Know My Own Strength" was still blaring through my headphones. I had to get my mind right before this session. I sat with my legs spread wide. My elbows rested right above my knees and my head was hung real low. My body rocked to the beat as my right foot passionately tapped to each cord. It was like I was preparing for a boxing match. "...I was not built to break..." Those words were burned in my brain.

From my periphery I saw Jason take a seat in front of me. Only his baggy blue jeans and white, red and black Asics were visible. I sensed that he was staring at me and trying to figure me out. Focus. I told myself. I will not crumble. My left fist was balled up and it pumped to the music when Denise said, "Vanessa?"

Apparently, Denise had called my name several times. I took the earphones out of my ears as I looked up to see her standing above me with her concerned eyes and said, "Are you ready?"

I took a deep breath and stood to my feet. I felt awkward as I followed her to the office, Jason just two steps behind me. I sat as close to the left arm of the couch as I could get. He sat to my right. Not to close.

Jason took in a deep breath and puffed his cheeks out as he let out a long breath and said, "Hello Vanessa."

Without looking in his direction I responded almost dead inside, "Hello."

I stared outside and watched the cars come and go into and out of the office park as Denise recapped with Jason what I had shared with her. I looked around her office as if it were the first time I'd been in there. There was a red and very comfy looking papasan chair in the opposite corner and a floor lamp with a cool looking beige shade. The walls were painted tan and lime green with a matching rug in the middle of the floor. Directly across from where I sat, behind her desk was a tan bookshelf. There were titles like "The Ethical Slut," "Opening Up," "Coming Out," and "Understanding Gender Dysphoria."

"Jason, do you understand why Vanessa is having such a hard time with this?" she asked.

He responded saying, "I do understand and I'm having a hard time too. Every married couple struggles with something. Why can't this be our thing? We took vows and said until death do us part."

My skin was boiling. So now he wanted to talk about vows? I turned and looked Jason in his eyeballs and very slowly and clearly stated, "This is like death Jason."

He got really quiet as I stared intently at him. He finally dropped his eyes and I whipped my head back around to look at Denise. Her eyes were sad. She said to Jason, "Do you understand that?"

After a long pause he responded saying, "Yes. I do," as he slowly nodded his head.

She began to address his childhood and how much of what he saw and didn't see around him could have played a major role in how he was currently feeling.

And then my ears were captivated by some of the most ridiculous words that I ever heard exit Jason's mouth, "There is nothing that I would change about Vanessa or our marriage. I love my life with her. I don't want to be without her. She is perfect for me. I'm ninety percent happy with my marriage and my life. But there is a void that makes up ten percent. I need to be free to date other women and build relationships with other women. It's not just about the sex."

My head turned so fast I should have gotten whiplash. I gave him a look of disdain as I cocked my neck to the side and nearly burnt a hole in his face. He didn't respond to the look. He just spoke some more gibberish, "I'm ninety eight percent sexually satisfied. But I can lay next to her after having mind blowing sex and two percent of me is unfulfilled."

I could hold my tongue no longer. I drew my neck back and spit fire out of my mouth as I enunciated my words clearly, "Are you fucking kidding me!?"

I threw my hands up as if to say I've had enough and I turned towards Denise. I twisted my lips and gave a look to say, "See this shit I was telling you about?"

He said nothing and Denise had a look of utter confusion on her face. I could see her trying to gather her words. "Well Jason...I'm concerned that you are going to fulfill the ten percent and knock off the bottom ninety percent." She paused, giving him time to speak.

"I feel encaged," he stated.

By then my nostrils were flaring and my chest was heaving. Denise said, "Breath through it like how I showed you."

With disgust I said, "I'm not having a panic attack. I just can't believe this bullshit that I'm listening to!"

"Ok. If you feel yourself about to have one start taking deep breaths," she instructed.

From the corner of my eye I saw him turn to me with concern. I said nothing. I just stared at her.

She then turned her attention back to Jason. "I'm concerned that you may not know what you're getting yourself into. You have a great marriage and a loving and supportive wife. People that come to me are not happy or something is missing with their partner. But there is nothing missing with your wife."

Yesterday she told me that she has lived with her wife for twenty years and the wife's girlfriend also lives with them. "Jason, I've been living this life for over twenty years. It's not easy. I date other people and they date other people. But my wife and I have to agree on the people that we date. Sometimes we have to tell each other no. This lifestyle is not easy. I'm just used to it."

"But there's other ways to do it," a classic Jason response. I threw my hands in the air and let out a breath of disgust. He always knew best. No one could ever tell him anything. And here we were. Our marriage was at a crossroads and as usual, if it didn't line up with his thoughts, then the other person just didn't know as much as he did. I was losing faith again.

Every day we went back and forth about this polygamous lifestyle that he wanted so badly. He would always say it's not a choice. And I would always tell him that everyone has choices and he was choosing to be selfish. I believed that his sexual desires were no different than any other mans but the difference was what he was going to do with his desires.

One evening I was sitting on the couch in the living room and he was sitting behind me at the kitchen table. The children had been laid down for bed and I decided to share a story with him. "I think it's totally normal for a man or woman who's been married for a long time to want to have sex with someone else. For me, that's not a problem and it's normal. The problem is when it's acted upon. There was a guy that I was friends with that I wanted to have sex with."

He straightened up and with total shock he said, "Jacob?"

I continued, "Yes. Jacob. But I knew that I didn't want to ruin my marriage for what would mean nothing at all. So I stopped all contact with him. It wasn't worth it. So, I understand how you started to develop a liking for Alley."

In one of our sessions with Denise he told me about an emotional affair that he had with his friend, Alley, five years back. I always suspected that he had feelings for her because he talked about her more than any of his other female friends. But I didn't want to rock the boat and start questioning things. What if I was wrong? I remembered one beautiful spring Friday I asked him if he wanted to go out after work. He was adamant that Friday's were his days to hang out with his friends. He refused to miss this Friday and I couldn't understand what the big deal was. He told me I was being unfair to ask him to miss his day out with his friends. I was so angry but he won. I later realized that he was just trying to get to her. When he told me about her in counseling I said, "I already knew that."

He was shocked that for once I didn't go off. I guess I needed my own experience so that I could understand his.

After I told him about Jacob he took a deep breath in, blew out and said, "Wow! I wasn't expecting that."

He paused and then continued on to say, "But I've been going over this in my mind for years and if I can have other partners then so can you. I know it will take some time but I will be ok with it. So you can call him up and do whatever you wanted to do with him."

I couldn't believe my ears. "Whatever Jason. You would not be ok with me having sex with someone else," I said.

"Yes Vanessa. I would be," he insisted.

"You can only say that because you know I'll never do it. You can imagine it in your head because you know that it's not real. The difference is when I imagine it, it is real. This is what you really want to do so it hurts like a pain that you will never understand," I said.

"You just don't understand," he said.

"No I don't. You have never even had a one-night stand Jason. You're not that guy. You never have been and now you have made it to 38 and you're ready to ruin your life for this. You're going to tear our family apart for this?"

"It's not a choice Vanessa. This is who I am and I'm not leaving you. I'm not going anywhere. I don't want our marriage to end," he insisted.

"Listen. I would not want you to leave me if I had of slipped up and had sex with Jacob. I would not want to end our marriage because of a mistake. I would want you to give me grace. Jason, I'm not saying that I want you to and many women would think I'm crazy for even saying this but I'm just being honest. If you have sex with someone else I won't leave you. I will give you grace. You can tell me and we can go to counseling and rebuild our marriage. I'm not letting you go because of that," I said with great compassion.

I felt like if he just had sex with one person it would be out of his system and then we could move on. As much as I didn't want to deal with infidelity, I felt like that's what was needed to fix us.

"Vanessa I'm not the best father or husband that I can be. I could be further along in my businesses if I had more freedom to be me and not think so much about what's wrong with me. I now realize that there's nothing wrong with me. I need freedom to go out with other women if I have a stimulating conversation with them. If I feel like I want to have sex with them I want to have the freedom to do that. If I want to take someone on a date because I want to get to know them better I want the freedom to do that," he said.

He stood there and shook his shoulders and said, "I need to be free. I appreciate you wanting to give me grace but I'll probably just sabotage our marriage some other way because I don't want to be with just one person."

"How do you know there isn't something wrong with our marriage? Why can't we dig deep into our marriage and see what's making you feel this way?" I asked. I was grappling for straws at this point.

He continued, "Vanessa, we both know there's nothing wrong with our marriage. Other than you not allowing me this freedom, you're perfect. You're the perfect wife for me. No one will ever hold me down like you do. I know that. I don't want us to change. I don't want to leave our marriage. I'm not going anywhere. I don't want you to leave me. I just need freedom."

Just then Reese came down the stairs and laid his head in my lap. We never argued around them but this night I had enough. In my mind we were getting divorced anyway so what did it matter. I guess he felt the same way because he continued on as if Reese were not there.

He asked, "Can't we have a "don't ask don't tell" policy? Two nights out of the week I'll go out and do me. We don't have to even talk about it."

My skin was scathing. I lifted Reese's head off of me and I stood up. I didn't know how to formulate my words. I poured myself a glass of water and began to drink it.

"This is not my choice Vanessa. It's just who I am," he said

"Everything is a choice Jason. We all have the freedom of choice. You are choosing this life," I yelled.

Everything inside of me wanted to hurl my glass at his head. From the corner of my eye I saw Reese resting his head on the back of the couch and watching the fiasco. I knew that if for no other reason I had to refrain for him. I slammed the glass on the counter, grabbed my keys and headed towards the door.

"Where are you going Mommy?" Reese asked.

"I'll be back," I answered angrily.

I peeled away in the car and before I could get off our street Joi was ringing my phone. "Yes!" I answered.

"Mommy are you coming back?" she asked.

"Yes. I won't be gone long," I responded.

She started crying and asked, "Where are you going?"

"I have to go baby. I'll be back soon. I love you," I said and hung up the phone.

I couldn't think straight but I knew that I shouldn't have left the house. I also knew that I couldn't compose myself inside the house. I felt like I did what was best for the moment.

About thirty minutes later I returned home. The children were awake but in their bedrooms. When I walked in the house Jason tried to tell me what was going on with the children when I left but I cut him off and with fire said, "Don't talk to me!"

I went upstairs to the children's rooms and told them I was sorry for leaving. I told them that I was upset and I just needed some air and there was nothing for them to worry about. I kissed them goodnight and went across the hall to my room.

I went to the bathroom to get myself ready for bed and I looked in the mirror. My face was scrunched up and my eyes looked tired and worn. I was tired. I didn't have much fight in me left. I didn't want to disappoint my children but I was killing myself in the process. I was losing the battle and it was time to let go. But I felt like I needed to keep fighting for my children's sake. The man that I married was lost and I couldn't bring him back but I had to keep trying because I didn't want my children to grow up in a one parent household. I had to try harder for them.

I sat in the bed for about an hour trying to figure out another angle to attack this. I began to bawl. I was losing and then it hit me. Jason had not seen me cry. He only saw me angry. He needed to see me cry. By now the children were asleep so I went downstairs so that he could see the pain, not anger that I was in.

He was sitting on the couch and turned around to the sound of my cries. I stood there vulnerable in front of him. I was letting him see my pain and hurt. Tears were pouring out of my eyes like buckets and my nose was stuffy from all of the crying. I said nothing. I just stood there looking at him. And then I started to point my finger vigorously at my chest and shrieked "You're killing me Jason! You're tearing our family apart!"

He stood up and started to walk near me. "Don't touch me!" I yelled as I backed away.

He leaned up against the island in the kitchen. His face also looked full of sorrow.

I continued to sob and I threw my arms out to my side, leaned in and asked, "What's worse Jason? Staying with me or being divorced but having your freedom?"

He shook his head and shrugged his shoulders and answered, "I don't know Vanessa."

I drew my neck back, cocked my head to the side, raised my eyebrows and gritted my teeth. With mass confusion in my voice I spewed out venom when I said, "You don't know!"

"I don't know Vanessa," he calmly repeated.

I turned towards the steps completely defeated. I went to the balcony off of our bedroom and started to meditate. Once again, I was crushed.

I talked to Kris several times a day, sometimes for hours. I shared everything with her but she was over 700 miles away. She suggested I start opening up to at least one or two friends that were nearby. But I was too afraid and ashamed, I guess, to tell anyone else. But she was right because I needed someone to talk to that I could look at and feel. I needed someone to sit with me and listen to me. I needed people to pray for us. Kris, Eric and Mimi prayed for us but I needed more. I finally worked up the nerve to ask Mona to come to my house so that I could tell her and ask for prayer. She was an awesome friend to me and so I knew she would be there for me and above all else I knew she would pray for us.

The children were staying with Mimi that evening and Jason was out driving Uber, so I was alone in an empty house. The silence was deafening and gave me chills. When the doorbell rang I felt instant relief and nervousness at the same time. I opened the door and Mona stood there. She was tall with a thin, fit frame. She had high cheekbones with perfectly clear caramel colored skin. There was a mole on her right cheek that added a special hint of beauty to her face. Her eyebrows were perfectly shaped above almond shaped eyes. I was never so happy to see her face.

"Hi," I said greeting her with a halfhearted smile.

She looked at me with a great deal of concern and hugged me. "Hi. What's up?" she inquired.

I motioned for her to follow me to the couch. She sat next to me as I looked down at my lap. I was trying to find the right words to tell her that my marriage was ending and I was crashing. "Well..." I couldn't get any other words out before I started crying.

She moved closer to me and put her arm around me. With her other hand she rubbed my leg. "Go ahead. It's ok," she said with a warm comforting voice.

"My marriage is ending. Jason wants to have an open marriage and I can't allow that," I managed to say.

"Oh no! You can't allow that. I'm so sorry. Where is this coming from?" She asked.

I proceeded to tell her everything and I shared with her one of my theories. He was always thinking about how to change

94

education, politics, and the world. He never relaxed his mind. Even when we were out on dates he would talk about all of his plans to make a difference in the world. He would rarely just "shoot the breeze" and always made sure that he was politically correct about everything. It even got to the point where he corrected me and all the people around him for not being politically correct.

I felt like he just needed to relax and get out more. I felt like he wanted this other lifestyle because he was seeking something different. Something exciting. I told her that I was going to suggest that he must go out at least once a week, every week, without me. He could flirt but that was it. And we were not to talk about anything serious while on our dates anymore.

She agreed that that could be the solution. I felt better and I was able to laugh again for the moment. She stayed for about an hour and a half and then she had to leave. I didn't want her to go because I knew that as soon as she walked out the door all of my doubt would come rushing back. I wanted to ask her to spend the night and it was on the very tip of my tongue to ask but I let her leave without asking. Plus, that would be very weird.

I dreaded night time because I couldn't sleep since all of this began four nights ago. I decided to make a run to the store to buy some Melatonin. On my way there I called Kris to let her know that I'd finally opened up. She was glad to hear that and asked where I was on my way to. I told her about my issues with sleeping and she suggested listening to a sleep meditation app.

When I returned home around ten I was excited to finally be able to get some sleep. I'd been walking around like a zombie and figured I'd at least feel a little better if I got a good night's rest.

I didn't know what time Jason would be home and didn't want to be awake when it happened. I felt like the later he came into the house, the greater chance there was that he had been frolicking with someone. I didn't know if he was driving for Uber or entertaining himself or someone else.

My plan was to go to sleep on the couch watching a movie with the lights off. I wasn't going to look at the clock if I happened to wake up and if I heard him come in I wasn't going to move a muscle. I had a solid plan.

I laid down after taking a melatonin. Sleep was about to happen and I couldn't wait. An hour later I was still awake. I started to get nervous that I'd be awake when he walked through the door. I didn't want to witness any evidence of gallivanting. I googled how much melatonin was too much and decided I'd take another one but this time I'd listen to the meditation.

Seventeen minutes passed and the meditation was over. I was still awake. I layed in the dark waiting for the big moment to fall asleep. I played the meditation again and I was still awake when it was over. Another hour had passed. I was so tired but like every other night, my body wouldn't shut down. I took a third melatonin and replayed the meditation again. At some point I finally drifted off to sleep and then the garage door opened, and Jason walked through the door. He poured himself a glass of water and took it upstairs. The water meant he'd been consuming alcohol. I started to think about what he'd gotten into for the evening but before I knew it I was back to sleep. Finally.

Every night for nearly three months were similar to that night. Thursday and Friday nights were the worst because those were the nights that he hung out in between driving. I would only fall asleep for brief periods of time and I would constantly look out the window every time I woke up to see if he'd come home yet. I was living in a sleepless nightmare for so many reasons. Lack of sleep was just one reason amongst many.

Each day that passed was worse than the next. I was broken. I was sad. I was angry. I was confused. I was anxious. I never knew what to do. I didn't know the answers. My chest ached constantly. I wanted so bad to just embrace him. I thought maybe that would make me feel better, but I never could. I thought I might drop of a heart attack at any moment. Often, I would put my hand over my heart hoping to ease some of the pain. Fearing that the worst was near. Fearing that the day would come when my heart would fail. I was afraid that my children would have to visit me in my hospital bed because I just could not get myself together. And the worst part was, I didn't know how to fix it.

One day in mid-August I was driving to work and, like so many mornings, I cried. I cried so hard that I couldn't wipe the tears away fast enough. I pleaded to God to help me. I pleaded that he would just give me a sign. Help me to make a decision. Show me the future. Something. I didn't want to make the wrong decision. Maybe there was something else that I could do that would help Jason. I pleaded with Him to change Jason's heart. I pleaded that He would help him to think clearly. Help him to see what he was going to do to our family.

As I neared work the tears would not stop. I drove into the parking garage still wiping them away. I sat for a few minutes and gave myself that all too familiar pep talk. Just pull yourself together long enough to get through the day, I told myself. I took some deep breaths. Told myself that I could do it. Looked in the trusty visor mirror, as I did so many times before, to make sure the evidence of sorrow wasn't apparent. And I got out the car, held my head high and got myself ready to pretend.

That day was particularly difficult because while I tried to take excellent care of my patients and function like a normal human being, I was also trying to decide which way to turn. By mid-day I had an answer. I decided that I was just going to let it all go. I was just going to move forward with my marriage and let the chips fall where they may. I could not bear the insurmountable stress anymore. I needed relief. I decided I would deal with whatever may happen, when it happens. At that moment, I finally felt some relief. I told myself, "Just deal with it later."

I was happy with my decision and so I called Kris on my way home to tell her. She said, "What does that mean?"

"I'm going to just let it go. I need a break. I feel like I'm going to drop of a heart attack at any moment. My stomach turns constantly. And even though I'm not having anxiety attacks anymore, I can feel the anxiety rise. I can't take it anymore. I'll deal with it when it becomes a problem."

As I heard myself say the words, "I'll deal with it when it becomes a problem," I realized how ridiculous that sounded. It's already a problem. And if I wait for him to tell me that he had sex with someone, then what? Panic took over again. My foot got heavy and I went flying through the traffic as I recounted all of the insanity that had occurred over the last 7 weeks.

I started to talk about the oddities of his relationship with Tina. I knew things didn't seem right between them but he insisted that their relationship was strictly professional. He talked about her way more than I was comfortable with.

He met her a year back when he was trying to get his school started. She showed an interest in his idea of a new way of learning and eventually became his business partner. Before June 26 I would ask probing questions about her and his relationship with her because of his frequent mentioning of her name. But they were questions that a man would never pick up on. In late July, I was driving home from work and decided at that moment that I had to know so I called him and made it very clear what I was asking. "What is your relationship with Tina?"

He responded quickly with, "She's my friend and business partner."

"Do you like her Jason?" I asked very sternly.

"No. She keeps it very professional. I love her like I love all of my friends," he said calmly.

"Let me tell you something about women's intuition. If you are being asked a question by a woman, please know that she already knows the answer. You have a ton of female friends and I've only felt this way about two of them. She is number two. And I was correct about number one. So, I don't care about all of your friends. I'm asking if you like, not love, her differently than you like your other female friends," I asked very irritated.

"I don't know about your intuition but I love her like all of my female friends," he said sticking to his original answer.

"You're lying Jason. And I've never known you to be a liar."

"Vanessa, I love all of my friends. I just love people. And I even tell my friends that I love them. Some of them think I'm weird and get uncomfortable. I…" I cut him off. Enough of the bullshit.

"You know what I'm asking you Jason! Do you like her differently?!" I enunciated the word "differently."

"Is there anything going on with us? No. Would I one day have sex with her or have a relationship with her in the future? I don't know Vanessa. I don't know what will happen in the future. I might develop a relationship with a parent at the school. I don't know." Now we were getting somewhere with his answer.

I was fired up and retorted, "See that's how bad you're blinded by this nonsense. You would actually have sex with her?! She's your business partner! If you weren't married and one of your boys asked you that same question, your answer should be absolutely not! Why?! Because you don't screw around with your business partner. And who the hell would get involved with a parent of the school? What the hell is wrong with you?"

"Vanessa, you know the life that I want to live but I will promise you this, I promise that I will never deal with her like that," he stated.

I didn't believe that for a second. I was sitting in traffic and I was riding my breaks because my mind was racing so fast that my foot was heavy on the gas. Every time I talked about this in the car I took a gamble. I may and may not crash into someone or something.

Tina had been to my home several times to work on details for the school. I welcomed her with hugs and kind words. The first time I met her I wondered if something in my home smelled bad because she had a turned-up nose that looked like something always stinks. She had a small gold hoop between her nostrils which didn't help the situation any. The nose ring reminded me of a bull. Her skin was a dark pretty shade of brown that was pleasantly complimented by her gold colored dreadlocks that hung slightly past her shoulders. I couldn't help but to notice the hair in her armpits which made me wonder if her legs where just as hairy. Her three-year-old daughter stuck close by her side. I wondered what her life story was because she moved here several months back from New York. She never did find a job and she was both car-less and phone-less and lived with her mom. Nonetheless, she was pleasant and seemed to be about her business.

During the summer while I was at work she would come over with her daughter while my children were there and she and Jason would work on the school details. I was about to bring that to a dead halt.

I composed myself and made sure I was crystal clear when I sternly said, "Tina is not welcome in my home anymore. She better not step a foot on my doorstep. Do you hear me? I better not look out my window and see her. She better not enter my block. Let me find out she's been in my home again."

"Ok. You don't want her in your face. I don't know how I'm supposed to tell her that. I don't want to even put out there that you're jealous. I don't want her to feel uncomfortable. She is my business partner." By now he was getting nervous.

"You don't have to tell her. I'll call her and tell her myself! And let me be clear...there is no jealousy here. I'm just not letting some chick that you're thinking about screwing, come into my home. There's a difference!"

Defeated and annoyed he said, "I'll handle it Vanessa."

Here's what I knew for sure. I was 40 with two children that I would die for if I had to. I wasn't about to start throwing fists like I'm an immature twenty-year-old. But if she were to cross my path I wasn't certain that the temptation to beat her face in wouldn't take over. So, I hoped the temptation was never tested.

So, as I spoke to Kris about Tina, it hit me. He was already in some type of relationship with her. He may not have been having sex with her but something was going on between them and I didn't need his words to confirm it.

My internal temperature started to rise. My heart started pounding and I began to shake. "Yo! This motha fucka has been messing with Tina all of this time!"

I started shaking my head back and forth vigorously. Kris just listened as I spewed out obscenities.

And at that very moment I came to a final decision. I'm done! I cannot be in this marriage anymore. I became very eager to end it but the caveat was that Heaven's Run was in two weeks and he had to be present. I was going to have family, friends and coworkers at the event. Even though I made my mind up, I wasn't about to tell the whole world so I decided I would hang on for just two more weeks. I was going to enjoy my time with my husband. I was going to be pleasant, have sex and be as normal as possible.

That decision gave me a resolved peace. I had a plan. Earlier that day I asked God to give me something. Anything. Help me to make a decision. He answered that cry. As I spoke to Kris He allowed me to clearly see that Jason had already started acting upon his new life of polygamy. He was doing it whether I liked it or not.

Chapter 5

The End is Near

Two weeks passed, and Heaven's Run was a major success and I was feeling great but totally exhausted. Set up started at 5am and I only had 3 hours of sleep so when the crowds left, I shut down. Joi and Reese were staying with Mimi for the rest of the day so that I could recuperate and Jason could go to work driving Uber. My friends wanted to go out to have lunch so I joined them but my mind was elsewhere. Aside from my body running on fumes, so was my mind. I knew that tomorrow my marriage might end and that's where my focus lay. I socialized with them for a bit and then I went home to rest. As I drove home I started to recount the day's events. Jason was always so proud of me for the work that I did with Heaven's Run. I started to think that he would be so proud of me that he wouldn't want to entertain any other women. I was both an amazing wife and person. I knew that and so did he. I couldn't imagine that he would turn all of this away for other women.

When I arrived home, he was already in a dead sleep in Reese's room. So, I layed down on the bed in our room with a smile on my face. I went to sleep thinking that everything would be ok with us.

About an hour later the scent of Jason's cologne filled my nostrils and jolted me out of my sleep as if a freight train came ramming through my home. My heart started to race and my breathing became heavy. Instant panic washed over me. Jason never wore cologne just to go driving. Was he going out with the intention of meeting someone? I thought all was going to be well between us.

He walked out of the bathroom and I lay perfectly still, all the while trying to slow my breathing down. I didn't want him to know I was awake. I was afraid to open my eyes and see what he was wearing. Was he dressed to impress? Sadness turned to anger again. All I could think about was ending this. I could not go another day with this constant turmoil taking over my life.

I heard the garage door open and I sat up. I wanted so bad to look out the window to see what he wore but I was too afraid to see. Now what do I do? I was back in full panic mode. So I decided to call him, thinking that somehow that would calm me.

"You're awake already?" He answered.

Not being totally forthright I answered, "I heard you leave and I couldn't go back to sleep."

"Oh man! I forgot to get a bottle of water. I'm going to turn around. Can you bring a bottle of water to me?' he asked.

My heart beat faster as I answered, "Ok."

I could no longer avoid seeing him. I was upset with myself for calling him but I got up anyway to walk the water out to him about 2 minutes later.

He had a huge smile on his face as I walked toward the car. The window was rolled down and he said, "I'm so proud of you. You did an awesome job today."

With a halfhearted smile I said, "Thank you."

I handed him the water and leaned in to kiss him. He was wearing blue jeans and his navy-blue polo shirt. The one with a big red polo logo on the left chest. He looked cute. Definitely cute enough to pick up some ladies if he wanted to. I took a quick inventory of the car. It was spotless as it usually was. There was nothing in there to tell me where he might be headed. We chatted for another minute or so and then he drove away. I told myself it was definitely time.

Later that evening I called him to ask him to come home. The anxiety was killing me. My stomach was in knots and I couldn't eat. I had to tell him. I couldn't wait until the next day.

"What time are you coming home?" I casually asked.

"I don't know. I'm going to stay out as long as I can to make up for the days that I missed," he answered. Totally unaware of what was about to happen.

"Can you come home early?" I asked.

With a chuckle in his voice he answered, "So that you can go to sleep on me? I really need to make up the time that I missed yesterday and today."

Fine! I thought. I needed to be clear headed for this conversation anyway. "Ok," I answered.

We got off the phone and I decided that it was time for my day to end. I took a shower and prepared my mind for tomorrow's conversation. I told myself that no matter what, I was saying the words "I'm done" on Sunday morning. I thought about the therapy session that I had with Calin earlier in the week.

Jason and I got to a point where Denise could no longer help us. By happenstance I met Calin at a social function one day and was instantly drawn to her, not even knowing that she was a couple's therapist. When I heard her talk about her line of work I exchanged numbers with her and called her later that day to see if she could help us.

Anyway, earlier in the week I told her that I was going to make him feel like shit. I was going to tell him that he's not shit and all of the reasons that he's a fucked up individual. I was going to drop him to his knees with my sharp words of hatred. This conversation was going to burn in his brain forever.

After I read her the very long list of topics that I was going to tear through she finally stopped me. She ever so gently shook her head from side to side. Her eyes looked sad. I could tell that she truly felt my pain and agony. "Do you think he already feels like shit Vanessa?" she asked me.

"Yup!" I proudly answered.

"So then why tear him down? That is what he's used to. Show him a side of Vanessa that he has never seen before. Keep it simple and calm. Do not engage in his conversation. State what you have to say and that's it," she advised.

I looked at her intentently. Then I cut my eyes to the left as I thought about what she was saying. She did kind of make sense. Just about every time Jason and I discussed any parts of the topic I ended up going off. My core was so damaged. My heart ached. My future was being ripped away from me. My children were going to be crushed. I was living in a state of constant anxiety. I could not help going off on him. But she was right. "Fine!" I said as I turned my eyes back to her.

After my shower that night I put the TV on and laid across the foot of the bed and drifted off to sleep. What seemed like a short time after, the garage door opened. Jason had returned home. I drifted back to sleep and then I awoke again to feel him cuddled against me. His chest lay flush against my back and his arm was wrapped around my waist. He gave me a gentle squeeze and kissed me on my cheek. I acted as though I was asleep and didn't feel any of that. But in reality, it felt so good. It reminded me of when we first met. We were not having sex but we would lay for hours just talking and getting to know each other. Falling in love. Now we were totally in love and with a family and he wanted to be free to like and love others. My temperature started to rise and eventually I drifted back off to sleep.

I layed still with my eyes closed when I woke up the next morning. I could tell that it was morning because I could hear the sweet melodies of the birds and I could see the light shining through my shut eyelids. But I did not dare open them. I needed time to get my mind focused and to figure out the proper words to use. "No backing out" I told myself over and over. I had no choice. I had exhausted all avenues of help. There were no more tricks up my sleeve to try and make us work. No backing out Vanessa. No backing out. No backing out. And then my eyes opened.

I lay motionless as I looked at Jason. He had a huge grin on his face as he said, "Good morning."

"Good morning," I whispered.

He looked so happy. His pillow was touching mine. I was reminded of the love that we shared as I looked at him. I always enjoyed waking up to him and just looking at him. Feeling joyous about whatever we were going to get into for the day. I wanted that back so freaking bad. Jason was truly my best friend and I was his. We were supposed to die together holding hands at 100 years old, for him, and 102 years old for me. I felt total bliss for most of our marriage. My heart sank.

Then he moved his head onto my pillow. Oh! How much I used to love that. We would fall asleep sharing the same pillow. And then when we woke up, one of us would move our head to the other pillow so that we were sharing once again. We would then embrace and greet each other with a kiss.

"How are you feeling?" he asked with a smile. It was as if we were not in the middle of sheer turmoil. Maybe he felt the same way I did yesterday. Maybe he thought I had a change of heart.

"Fine," I tried to give the answer some life.

"The children aren't here. Wanna have some morning fun?" He asked full of giddy referring to having sex.

The moment was here. No backing out I told myself. "No," I responded and then took a deep breath and said, "I want to talk."

His demeanor immediately changed. His smile left his face and a serious Jason asked, "Ok. About what?"

"Us," I responded. My mouth was getting dry and my underarms were getting moist.

He let out a long sigh and sat up. He leaned his back against the headboard. The sun was shining bright because even though the blinds were still shut, the baby blue walls of our bedroom lit up. The king-sized deep cherry headboard looked giant against him. For just a brief moment I thought about the day we purchased our bedroom furniture. We were newly married and excited about moving to Georgia. We picked out only the best furniture to fill our brand-new home.

Anyway, I cut my eyes to the bathroom which was adjacent to the bedroom. It was bright inside as if the light was on but it was just the sun peeking through the window.

"Ok. I knew this had to come," he said.

He'd been asking for the last 3 or 4 weeks if we could talk about us and I kept telling him that I needed to get through the run first.

"I'm no longer willing to discuss anything else if we are not discussing me and you. I am not entertaining conversations about other women any more. If it is not me and you then I am done," Just like that. I said it. Calmly. I didn't even feel a need to be loud. My words screamed for me.

Calmly and calculated he responded, "I wish you could be in my head. I love you so much and it's not you…"

I cut him off and shook my head back and forth, "No more. I cannot do it. I cannot hear not one more time about what's in your head. I am done. I want you to move out." I took a deep breath. "And I want you to move out today."

"Vanessa. I wish you would just read the article that I sent you," he halfway pleaded. He sent me an article to read about 3 weeks back about people 'like him'. How they are capable of romantically loving more than one person.

With a calm resolve I said, "No more Jason. I will not read not one more article. I have constant anxiety. My stomach turns all day and all night."

He interrupted with, "So does mine."

"I have lost sixteen pounds. I feel like I'm literally going to have a heart attack on most days. I will not do it anymore. I'm done. I want you to move out today."

Calmly and confidently he said, "This is my home too and I'm not moving out. And I'm not leaving my children."

Once more I calmly stated, "I want you to leave today."

"I'm not leaving Vanessa," he responded.

I got off the bed and said nothing. I was calm and felt in control of my emotions for once. I walked into the bathroom and turned the shower water on. I closed the door behind me and proceeded to brush my teeth and then I stepped into the shower. I'm not really sure how I felt. It was very strange. I wasn't crying. I didn't even feel the need to cry. I suppose because I had already cried a thousand times for this day. I was thankful for Calin's advice. Peaceful was definitely better. It showed that I have moved to another dimension in my feelings.

From the shower I started to hear Jason coughing. Why is he coughing like that I thought? It was fierce. I started to get nervous. Did he do something to himself? I wondered if I needed to check on him. Before I could decide the bathroom door opened. He was crying deep down from his gut. His cries filled the empty space in the bathroom as the sounds of his pain bounced off the walls. He tore off a piece of toilet tissue and blew his nose. He continued to cry as he walked back out.

At that moment I didn't feel bad at all. I knew that I did all that I could to keep us together. I loved us but we ended the moment that he made up in his mind that there was nothing wrong with him and what he was requesting was totally normal. I could not comfort him and I had no words for him.

After my shower I got dressed and walked downstairs. Jason was sitting on the couch watching ESPN. In total silence I grabbed my car keys and left the house. I spent the rest of the day driving around in the car, sitting in the car at the park, listening to music and talking out what had just happened with Kris, my parents, Mimi and my good friend, Tosha. He texted me asking if we could get together the next day to discuss how to split things and visitations with the children. Damn! That seemed so cold but no tears fell that entire day. I was totally numb. I was hoping he'd tell me that he can't live without me. But instead he couldn't live without them. Those women.

After many hours of sitting in the car I drove to Mimi's house to pick up the children and then I headed to my parents' house. I decided the children and I would stay there for the night.

The next morning, I went to my session with Callin. She asked me how I felt and I told her that I felt relieved. Relieved because the weight of the unknown had been dropped. But still, there were many unknown factors. I prayed that reality would hit him once he moved out. I prayed that that would knock him to his senses.

After the session he and I met at our house. I was so sad. At that moment I wasn't even angry. Just so very sad. Upon walking in the house there was a heavy, glum feel. Our house was always so full of love and happiness. As I sat on the far end of the couch I thought about when we first moved in and made our house a home. I looked at the huge wooden Roman numeral clock that sat in the nook above the fireplace and TV. I remembered loving that clock so much that I had the walls of the living room, dining room and sitting rooms painted crimson and tan just so the clock would stand out.

I looked into the kitchen at the mustard colored walls. I always admired the colors of our home. They made me feel warm. We had an open floor plan so the kitchen flowed right into the living room. I wanted it that way so that when we would have company over no one had to choose which room to be in. We both loved entertaining friends and family in our home so this was the perfect layout for us. But on that day, our house was shut in and cold in the middle of the summer.

He sat at the kitchen table, right behind the couch. The computer was set up so that he could document this budget meeting. Is this all he thought about that night? The budget and how to split everything up? My heart broke a little more.

"Are you divorcing me?" he asked.

I responded, "I think we first need to separate."

I was hoping this would shake him up enough for him to make a better, wiser decision.

"So we need to decide what to do with the house and a plan for the children," he said very businesslike. I couldn't look at him. I just sat sideways, towards him, looking out of the window.

"I'm staying in the house and the children will be with me," I spoke softly.

"Can you afford the house and all of the bills?" he challenged me.

I had no idea if I could. These were not the things that I thought about after parting with him yesterday. Nonetheless, it didn't matter. The bills were not going to keep me as his wife. I shrugged and a deflated voice said, "I'll figure it out."

We sorted through some other things and agreed that we would each have fifty percent of responsible custody of the children. When we finished there were no parting words. I just walked out the door.

At some point really soon, the children had to be informed of the new life that they were about to live. I stayed at my parents' house with the children the next two nights because I could not bear to go home. I couldn't face that reality. By the third night Joi was asking questions because she needed to know why we were not sleeping at home. I would respond by asking her what's wrong with staying there. I told her it was easier for me to stay there and go to work the next morning then have me or Jason take them in the morning. I knew she was suspicious but that was the best reasoning that I could come up with.

On Wednesday, Jason was going to be with the children all day. He sent me a text the night before saying that he was going to tell the children because he just couldn't hold it any longer. "The hell he is! He will not tell them in the absence of me," I said to myself.

So, I responded saying I'll facetime him and we can tell them. I knew that was not the right approach but my heart started racing just thinking about being in his presence. Of course, he quickly responded saying that he can't do it like that and so I asked him to come over.

My underarms started to sweat as I anticipated his arrival and breaking the news. I told Joi and Reese that Daddy is coming over and then I walked into my parent's room to tell them. I whispered because I didn't want the children to hear. My mother pretty much rolled her eyes as I told them and my father just calmly said, "Ok."

Several minutes later the doorbell rang. My heart began to pound and instant anger washed over me. I really just wanted to beat his head in. I couldn't believe that he was really going through with this. He was really about to tear our family apart for this lifestyle. A lifestyle that he didn't even know if he would like. My breathing get heavier and I started to see rage in front of me. In my head I was cursing him but I had to remain calm. At this moment, all that mattered for me were my children. I had to remain calm for them.

My parents didn't come out of their room and I wasn't about to open the door. "Answer the door. It's your father," I said trying to hide the hatred in my voice.

Both Joi and Reese ran to the door. They had not seen him in two days. "Daddy!" They both shouted happily.

His voice was very subdued as he responded, "Hello."

They exchanged pleasantries and then he told them that we had to talk to them. He looked at me and motioned towards the basement door. "Do you want to talk down there?" he asked.

I mumbled gibberish under my breath and proceeded to walk downstairs. Being in the basement at my parents' house was always a fun time. That meant we were watching movies under the starry ceiling in the theater room, having a big family dinner, having a birthday party for the children or watching the children run in and out of the basement door in the summer time as they enjoyed backyard fun. All pleasant memories. But not this evening.

The basement was always brightly lit but this evening it seemed strangely brighter. The silence was deafening as we all sat down on the couch. I sat at the edge of one couch while Jason took a seat on the other couch where the two couches joined. Joi sat between us and Reese sat on the other side of Jason. I scooted closer to Joi because I knew she was going to need comforting.

I absolutely refused to be the one to tell them about our separation. This was his doing so he was going to have to tell it. I rested my elbow on my knee and placed my chin in my hand. My hand covered my mouth and nose because I didn't want my anger to show. I burned a hole in Jason's face as I stared at him waiting to speak.

He took a deep breath in, breathed out heavily and proceeded with the words, "Mommy and I are separating. We aren't able to agree on our marriage so we are going to live apart from each other. We both love you..."

As he spoke I began to shake. I was searing with anger and my face was crunched tight behind my hand. I couldn't believe what I was hearing. My leg shook vigorously. It was the only thing that stopped me from showing out in front of my children. For a moment I got light headed. I felt like I could tip over at any time.

Joi began to cry forcefully. I was so angry that I couldn't even comfort her. I was using all of my energy to stop myself from beating the life out of Jason. His eyes began to swell with tears and the words almost escaped my lips, "What the fuck are you crying for!?!?!?" But instead, I scooted closer to Joi until my thigh rested next to hers. I put my arm around her and leaned her in close to me. I couldn't take my hand from off my face. I couldn't even speak. I just held her.

"I'm sorry Joi," Jason said.

My thought, "You mother fucking bastard! Fuck you bitch!"

By this time Reese was sitting on the couch upside down with his legs flailing in the air. I shot my eyes at him but didn't say a word. "Sit up buddy," Jason said.

He sat up and asked, "So you are going to live somewhere else and we will see you on the weekend like Chase and Amber?"

Chase and Amber lived with their mom but their dad lived across the street from us. They were the ages of Joi and Reese and played with them often. "Yes. That's what it will be like," Jason answered.

"I'm ok with that, "Reese responded so carefree.

He had turned five years old a few months back and couldn't understand the gravity of what this meant. Jason chuckled and on any other day I would have found that funny too but not today. I just looked at him as I continued to embrace Joi. Leg still shaking.

Joi asked questions and Jason answered them. Then she asked, "Will we still have Sunday dinner together?"

"If Mommy lets me," he responded.

I chimed in, trying so hard to hide my hate, "We will have to see."

"Will you be friends?" she asked.

"Hopefully one day Mommy will want to be friends with me," Jason answered.

What the fuck was wrong with him? Why was he putting this on me? I had to think quickly. "Yes. One day we'll be friends."

She started crying fervently again. Jason put his arm out gesturing for her to come near. I let go of her and she scooted over to his arm. He hugged her and said sorry and told her how much he loved her. Meanwhile, Reese was just watching his sister cry as if he wasn't bothered at all by the news.

Joi asked some more questions and then Jason told them again that he loved them and said he was going to go. We all walked up the stairs quietly. Jason hugged and kissed them and told them goodnight. Then I said, "I'll walk you to the door."

"Ok," he responded.

As we walked towards the door I envisioned me kicking him in the ass so hard that his back broke. But, of course, that wouldn't sit well with my children. He opened the door and said goodnight. I said nothing in return. He walked out the door and I quickly put my hand on the handle to pull it shut. Before his foot hit the first stair I had both doors closed and locked. Under my breath I said, "Get the fuck outta here!"

I was so full of anger that I didn't know what to do with myself. I hugged my children tight and told them to get ready for bed. I needed to vent but I couldn't because I didn't want them to hear me so I sent Kris multiple texts asking her if it was ok for me to call him and tell him he's a piece of shit. She told me it served no purpose and that I am sowing seed in the ground for my harvest. She told me to hold it together for my children and to focus on my healing. She said he really doesn't feel remorse. That stung but it was true. He didn't. She metaphorically talked me down and back into calmness.

After we were all ready for bed I laid between my babies on the full size bed. There wasn't much room for all of us but they wouldn't let me sleep in the other room by myself and really, I didn't want to be by myself. I wanted to be right there with them.

I told them how much I loved them and I promised them that we would all be ok. I assured them that they would always have me and that I would never leave them. I told them that life will be good and we will live an amazing life together. I believed that. I just needed to first get myself together.

Joi started to get on Reese for not caring. Then Reese said, "I do care Joi."

And then he needed reassurance, "Will we live with you?"

"Yes son," I responded.

My heart ached but I was thankful to have my babies next to me. I kissed both of them and told them goodnight. I lay on my back so that I could be equally close to both of them. Joi wrapped her arm around my stomach and snuggled her head on me. Reese took my arm and layed it across his pillow. Then he faced me and laid his head on my arm. My heart was heavy but full of joy in that moment.

That next morning my alarm rang after what seemed like only minutes of rest. I very quickly turned the alarm off, got up and took my clothes to the bathroom. I was brushing my teeth when I heard a light knock at the door. I opened the door to see Reese rubbing his eyes. "Good morning son. You can go back to bed. I'm getting ready for work and I'll tell you goodbye before I leave."

He said nothing but came into the bathroom and laid down on the bathroom rug. "I'm about to take a shower. You can't be in here while I shower."

Then Joi appeared at the door. "Good morning baby," I said greeting her.

"Good morning. Can I come in?" she asked

I gestured for her to come in. Reese sat up and Joi took a seat on the floor near him. I squatted down between them. I didn't know what to say but I was getting teary eyed. Then I looked at Joi and said, "We are going to be ok. I promise."

Then I turned and looked deep into Reese's eyes. He's not a kid that verbalized emotion but his actions and nonverbal cues spoke volumes. His eyes looked sad and scared. My emotions got the best of me and I began to cry. "I promise. We are going to be ok." I assured him.

Then I put an arm around both of them and held them close. I rested my head on Reese's head. "I promise I will never leave you...You will always have me...We will be ok. I promise...I promise."

I continued to weep as I held them. Then I stood up and ran the shower water. They both laid down on the floor. Not saying a word. I took my pajamas off and got in the shower and cried and cried. I thought to myself, my children are five and nine and here I am taking a shower in front of them because their father wants to have relations with random women. I was too sad to be angry. I just wanted my children to be ok.

After I got out of the shower and got dressed Joi and Reese followed me throughout the house as I gathered my belongings and got my breakfast together. Then I told them goodbye and Reese started crying and through his tears he said, "I don't want you to go. Why do you have to go to work?"

My heart was torn. My mother came out of her room to help. I gave him one last hug and was going to walk out of the door but he wouldn't let me go. He had a tight grip around my neck. So tight that it began to hurt. "Mommy can you get him off of my neck," I managed to say.

With much effort she was able to pry him off of me. I kissed and hugged Joi, told them both that I loved them and walked out the door.

Then I made my daily Monday through Friday call to Kris. I started to tell her about what occurred after we finished texting each other last night and what happened this morning. As I recounted the events I began to cry. "He's messing with my babies. Nobody messes with my babies," I said.

She went on to soothe me by speaking positively. She told me she was proud of me for not going off on him the night before. She was definitely my rock. Several minutes later our conversation ended. I cried some more and then I had to clean my face up and put on my game face because work was awaiting me.

At work I couldn't stop thinking about how that all went down. I just wanted my children to be whole. I didn't want them to be broken like me. And I didn't want them to think that I was the one hurting them. I needed them to know that it wasn't me without saying it was Daddy. I couldn't focus anymore at work and I called my father and said, "Can you please let them know that I didn't do it. I don't want them to know what happened but I want them to know that it wasn't my fault. I don't want them to be mad at me."

Every day my heart broke some more and my parents were watching me crumble. "I will talk to them," he assured me.

Thirty minutes later the children were ringing my phone. I answered with a hello and Reese said, "If Daddy didn't want to be married why did he marry you?"

Before I could respond to that Joi said, "Why doesn't Daddy want to stay married to you? Pop Pop said you tried your best to keep the marriage together. He said you even went to counseling. He said you didn't put him out but he didn't want to stay."

"Mommy why did Daddy marry you if he didn't want to be married?" Reese repeated.

My senses were on overload and I didn't know how to handle the situation so I just started crying. Silently. I didn't want them to think they caused my tears.

Completely defeated I said, "I don't know son. That's a question for your father."

"Well why didn't he want to stay Mommy?" Joi repeated.

"I don't know. I'm sorry baby," I responded.

I tried to speak words of comfort to them and asked them to try and not focus on it. I assured them again that we would be ok and then I got off the phone with them.

After work I went to counseling with Calin. "How are you?" she asked.

I shook my head. I told her about the recent events and then I said, "I'm so upset with my father. He shouldn't have told them that. That's not what I asked him to tell them."

She put me in check real quick. She said, "Hold on now Vanessa. You asked him to tell them it wasn't your fault. What did you think you he was going to tell them? You're his baby and he doesn't care as much as you do about them finding out the truth and you know that. He told you before that they need to know the truth. So, what did you think he was going to tell them?"

I looked at her and shrugged my shoulders and said, "I get your point."

"You wanted him to tell them and then he did and you got upset. This isn't his fault Vanessa. This is your doing," she said very matter of factly.

She paused so I could digest what she was saying. I just looked at her with an uncomfortable smirk on my face.

She went on to say, "If it's your father's fault then it's also your fault for marrying Jason and Eric's fault for introducing you two."

"You're right," I said.

It wasn't my father's fault and I guess in some way I did want him to tell them. Either way, it was already done and it was now my job to manage it.

The rest of that week was rough to get through. The children were asking questions of me, Jason, Pop Pop and Mimi every day. They would ask things like is daddy a bad person? Why is everyone upset with him? For me those were very difficult questions because although I hated Jason, I really didn't want to implicate him as a bad person to my children. On the other hand, Pop Pop was willing to tell it all if pushed far enough. He didn't curtail his answers and so I had to word my answers to the children to make everyone look good without making anyone look bad. That was exhausting.

At the end of the week I was driving home from work and Jason called me and said he was going to get me back. I figured I could at least listen to this plan but I wasn't hopeful. "I'm working on a plan to get you back. I'm still in love with you and I don't want to lose you. I'll tell you about it tomorrow," he said with both excitement and nervousness in his voice.

The next morning came and Joi came bouncing down the steps with a vibrant smile. She was so beautiful. She had rich chocolate colored skin with a hint of red undertone. She had big bright eyes that made her face shine. Her eyebrows were also thick like mine, Jason and Reese's. Her body was tall and slender like I was growing up. "Here Mommy. Daddy asked me to give you this," she said.

It was an envelope that read 'For better or for worse…to Vanessa with LOVE.' I was immediately angered that he would have Joi deliver a letter to me with that caption. I immediately recognized that he was manipulating the situation.

I thanked her for the letter and she asked with excitement, "Are you going to open it?"

"Later," I said.

When the house was empty later that day I opened the letter. He broke down his feeling's day by day since the day I told him 'no more.' He spoke of needing me in his life and not being ready

134

to lose his best friend and soulmate but not wanting to lose himself either. He didn't want to live apart from his children but what was he to do. He said he wanted me to have grace and accept him for who he was. So, his plan was to fight for me and shower me with unconditional love.

I threw the letter and said out loud, "This is some bullshit! This is his plan? This is the same shit just written on paper!"

I could see so clearly that he needed to address the source of his feelings which had nothing to do with me. He needed to address his childhood. Did not seeing any positive role models other than his grandparents who lived almost 1,000 miles away cause some of this? Or not having his mom and dad together and all that came along with that? Maybe the fact that he never saw himself different than the common man when it came to sex? Possibly because his mom still looked out for his dad even though they were divorced? Maybe he was afraid to fully commit his life to one person because growing up he never saw the benefits.

Either way, he was going to throw everything away for nothing. His letter only hurt me further.

The next day he had Joi deliver another letter that was titled on the envelope, 'To the love of my life, Vanessa.' I hesitantly took the letter from her and said, "Please do not take any more letters from Daddy for me. If he wants to give me a letter, tell him that Mommy prefers for him to hand it to her himself. Tell him that I will not take any more letters from you."

With sadness she said, "I'm sorry Mommy. I…"

I interrupted her saying, "I'm not upset with you baby. It's not your fault. You are not in trouble. I just prefer Daddy to give me his own letters."

I gave her a hug and told her how much I love her. And then I sent him a text to not ever send another letter through her again.

After he left the house that day Joi said, "Why are you mad at Daddy?"

I just looked at her and gave no response.

"He said he's going to get you back. He said he's going to do everything that he can to keep you as his wife," she said so innocently.

I was burning hot. How dare he use my children in that way and make me look like the bad guy. Like I'm the one tearing our family apart. I could hold my tongue no longer. I looked Joi square in the eyes and as stern as I could be I said, "I'm going to be honest with you Joi. I don't care what Daddy tells you. More than likely we are going to get divorced."

Her big beautiful eyes were lowered to the ground and her lips started to frown. I continued to say, "I know you don't like that and I'm sorry. But I'm being honest with you. This will probably end in divorce."

She began to sob. I felt horrible but I didn't know what else to do. He was giving them false hope and it was all falling on me. I hugged her long and tight. I kissed her cheeks and her forehead. I tried to wipe away her tears but they just kept falling. I felt so hurt for her but I was too angry to cry.

Three weeks passed and Jason was still living in the home. I asked him not to sleep in our bedroom and to use the children's bathroom until he moved out. I know longer wanted him in my intimate corners. He agreed and said he would live in the playroom until he moved out.

I wanted him to leave. I needed him to leave. I could not look him in the face and it was too painful to be in his presence on the rare occasions that we were home at the same time. I was too angry to part any words to him. Even hello and goodbye. So, I just ignored his existence. I knew that seeing us together but unloving was no good for Joi and Reese.

So, on a Sunday afternoon, three weeks after I asked him to move out, we had another meeting in the home without the children's presence. My eyes were fixed on the chair that he sat in as I said, "It is not healthy for the children to see us like this and I don't like seeing you. I'm sure you don't like being around me either. It is best for all four of us if you move out. When are you leaving?"

He let out a deep sigh and said, "I was told that if I leave then I will be considered abandoning the children and I could lose all of my rights to them."

I lifted my face to him and looked him in the eyes for the first time in three weeks. He looked different to me. Like I didn't know him. His eyes were sad and his face looked worried. He was growing his beard out. It was salt and pepper colored with much more salt than pepper. He was rough looking.

I very matter of factly stated, "If that's why you're staying then you can leave. They are your children too and I would never take them from you. You can come over and see them whenever you would like."

Shortly after our initial meeting I told him that I know longer was ok with 50/50 custody. I didn't think the constant back and forth from house to house was best for them. I told him that they could stay with him every other weekend but they were going to live with me from Sunday to Friday. He told me to lawyer up because he wasn't about to pay for two households and never be able to get forward financially. I wasn't moved and told him to let me know when. When never came. I was going to be the primary parent.

"So now when are you leaving? I'll even help you," I boldly stated.

I could tell that I made him very uncomfortable. He was not used to this side of me and he didn't know how to handle me. I backed down to nothing and I think sometimes it shook him to his core. He responded saying, "Then I'll be gone by Tuesday, Wednesday. I'll start packing tomorrow. If you really want to help me then you can buy some boxes for me."

"I can do that," I said full of sarcasm.

He said, "Thank you," and then he asked, "What do you tell people?"

In an even more sarcastic tone I looked him in the eyeballs again and said, "Exactly what you tell me. Whatever you tell me. That's what I tell people."

"Moving forward I would like you to tell people that we grew apart," The words came out confident but I think he'd lost his mind. He didn't get that I was no longer his wife. I didn't do whatever was best for him anymore. I was only out for self and my children.

With a sharp tongue I retorted, "I will not tell people that! We did not grow apart! I'm gonna tell them what you tell me." I stared at him and cocked my head to the side with my arms folded.

His demeanor was of one whose back was up against a wall. His legs were halfway crossed and his elbow rested on his knee. His hand was on his chin and he slowly shook his head up and down as if he was trying to absorb what I'd just said. He was looking away from me and bit the corner of his bottom lip like he always did when he was in deep thought.

140

"Ok," there was a long pause, "Ok. I'll have to speak on it one day anyway. I'm gonna write a book about it." He tried to be calm, but I could tell he was shook.

I responded with a simple and unbothered, "Ok."

Then we discussed exactly how we were going to handle the bills once he moved out. I was so disgusted sitting there looking at him. I wanted to spit in his face. I started to ball up my fist. I envisioned me kicking him out of the chair and then beating his face in with my fist until I fell over from exhaustion. The longer I sat there, the angrier I became. I almost swung my fist at his face but I kept telling myself, "Don't do it Vanessa. Don't do it. Don't do it. Calm down."

I couldn't take it any longer and I forcefully pushed my chair back from the table and got up. I began to walk towards the bathroom that sat adjacent to the kitchen. He said, "The other day you said I never said sorry. I'm sorry Vanessa. I'm truely…"

I closed the bathroom door on his words as I said a lifeless, "Whatever."

After all necessary details were discussed I picked up my car keys and left the house fuming hot. My blood was boiling when I closed my car door. "I can do you one better than that! I'll pack ya shit for you and you're getting the fuck out of here today!" I yelled out loud. With every minute that passed I drove faster and faster. My foot was heavy on the gas as I cursed him all the way to Wally World.

Ten minutes later I whipped my car into a parking spot and hopped out the car on a serious mission. I grabbed a shopping cart and plowed through the aisles in search for the biggest storage bin I could find. My lips were tight, teeth clenched, nostrils were flaring and my breathing was heavy and deep. Smoke was probably coming out of my nostrils as I mumbled all kinds of profanity. My thoughts were so loud that innocent bystanders could probably hear them.

When I finally came across the bins I started to get angrier. I snatched the thirty-gallon bin and dropped it in my cart. By now my face was completely distorted and I dared anyone to look at me cross eyed. I wanted a reason to break someone's back and I was ready to throw down. I didn't want anyone to ask me how I was doing or was I ok so I went through the self-scan line to avoid any unnecessary conversations.

I flew through the streets to get back home. Jason was gone and I practically ran up the stairs to our bedroom to pack his shit.

"You wanna fuck some other chicks mother fucka?! Fuck you bitch! Get the fuck outta my house you sorry ass mother fucka!"

By now I was shouting with thick white spit flying out of my mouth. My head was flipping from side to side as I tried to catch my breath in between shouting obscenities.

Twenty minutes later half of the bedroom was packed in the bin. Not one single item of his was left unpacked. Then I stood there looking at the bin, completely out of breath. I threw my hands up and with complete annoyance said, "How the fuck am I gonna get this downstairs!"

"This is some bullshit!" I said as I struggled to push the bin down the hallway. When I got to the top of the stairs I stood up, put my hands on my hips and contemplated how I would get the bin down the stairs without it flipping over. I wiped the sweat off my face with the back of my hand causing it to run down my arm. Like a child, I wiped my arm on my t-shirt and commenced to carefully dragging the bin down two flights of stairs.

Once I reached the bottom of the stairs I thought I was in the clear until I pushed it out to the car. I let out a deep breath of frustration as I stared into the back seat. "How the fuck am I gonna get this in the car," I said out loud. Not caring if the neighbors were watching.

I went back in the house to get a sheet to lay on the back seat. Then I squatted real deep, got my fingertips under the bin, took a deep breath, lifted and tilted the bin up and with my knees I pushed it forward to lean it on the top of the seat. "Fuck! My back," I said.

I straightened up and put my hands on my lower back. I arched my back and leaned my head backwards as I tried to work the kink out. Then I let out a deep breath and pushed it the rest of the way in and slammed the car door to solidify a job well done.

My clothes were soaked and the smell of my sweat was invading my nostrils. I went back inside and packed up all of the pictures of us that sat for our guests to see. I left the large wedding picture on the wall because I knew Joi would be hurt if it were missing. I threw the pictures along with some other odds and ends into the car and then I took a quick shower.

I drove five minutes around the corner to Mimi's house to unload Jason's shit. I called Mimi on my way there so I knew no one was home. All of his belongings were awaiting him as soon as the front door was opened to his new two-bedroom apartment shared with his mom and his brother, Drew. "Let's see how much ass you get living here asshole," I said as I walked back to my car.

I took a seat and texted him: "You can start staying at your mom's apartment tonight. All of your belongings are there. Everything that you will need over the next few days can be found on top."

I looked at the time and only two hours had passed from the end of our meeting. I'm sure this was yet one more thing that had him shook.

Every time my phone would ring with his name or a text or email came through from him I would experience anxiety. My underarms would begin to sweat, my heart would begin to race and my breathing would become a little heavier. I never know what he wanted or what would be in his messages and I never knew how I was going to respond to them. So I would read and listen to his messages when I felt like I was ready to be confronted with whatever he had for me that day.

Now that we didn't live together anymore it was harder than ever for him to get in contact with me because I no longer felt obligated to entertain his nonsense. I told myself that I would be calm when dealing with him no matter what he said. But on this particular day I had something to say and was ready for a fight.

His phone rang and I went in. "You know what? You don't know anything about sacrificing. You say that you sacrificed for six years by suppressing your feelings and going to counseling while all along you were going to counseling but just waiting for me to change my mind. That's not trying and sacrificing. That's you doing what you needed to do until I changed my mind and got on board with you."

"Vanessa where is this coming from. I answered the phone and you're attacking me," he said with confusion.

"You said you sacrificed by driving extra to pay for my birthday party. Are you kidding me? You sacrificed for a party that I truly enjoyed and appreciated. But I sacrificed and provided a lifestyle for you. An entire lifestyle. I wanted to be a stay at home mom after Joi was born and I sacrificed. You could have taken on another job but instead you told me that I could stop working if we moved to an apartment. It wasn't convenient for you to do more so you didn't. Then after Reese was born you said you didn't want to work a nine to five anymore. You said you needed freedom to work for yourself and so I held down a job and benefits while you attempted to pursue your dreams. That's real sacrifice. Not working extra to pay for a party," I stated all of the facts and then he interrupted me.

"I did sacrifice Vanessa…" he said as I cut him off.

"No, you didn't. You don't know anything about sacrificing. You chose yourself over our children. You told me that you needed to save yourself. When you become a parent it's no longer about you. You don't leave your children to save yourself!" By now I was shouting but I was trying to reel myself back in.

"I didn't want to leave. I said I wasn't going anywhere. You put me out. I didn't want to leave Vanessa so stop saying that I left you and the kids. I didn't leave them," he tried to defend himself.

"You left our marriage the moment you decided that you want to live this other lifestyle. I lived up to our vows. You tried to change them and then expected me to accept that. Don't try to twist this. You left the marriage when you made your choice," I said not backing down.

"And stop saying it's a choice. It's not a choice. I can't help who I am. I told you when we got married that if I ever felt like I wanted to have sex with someone else I would tell you," he said trying to defend himself again.

147

I was vexed now and I was spitting fire, "Telling me that you will let me know and then actually wanting to live this lifestyle are two different things Jason. Stop trying to fall back on that. Being honest and telling me is not the same as what you are doing. And I even gave you a pass to have sex with someone else and that wasn't good enough. You always want more! Nothing is ever enough for you! Who the fuck is 98% sexually satisfied and complains? You need to figure out the real root of your issues!"

"I'm sorry that I hurt you. I'm hurting too. I just love you so much that I had to be honest with you," he was pleading for my sympathy.

I rolled the windows up and shouted as loud as my voice would go, "Don't you ever say you love me! Ever again! Don't you ever, ever, ever, ever, ever, ever, ever, ever, ever, ever, ever, ever, ever, ever, ever, ever, ever, ever, ever, ever say you love me ever again! Not ever!"

My entire body was shaking and I felt like my head was going to explode.

Forcefully he said, "It's an orientation Vanessa. Just like being straight or gay is an orientation. Being polyamorous is an orientation. I found a support group and I wish you would come…"

I cut him off with a sharp tongue, "I'm not going nowhere!"

"Vanessa there are couples there just like us but they are making it work. And I'm envious of them. After hearing some of their stories I realized that you just don't have the emotional capacity to love…" I stopped his words.

"Fuck you!" I roared.

Finally he'd had enough and hung up. And I was sizzling. I didn't know what to do with myself so I just sat there until I calmed down.

The next morning, I felt regret for the way that I spoke to him. I had never used such venom with him before and I felt bad for getting so far out of control. I sent him a text apologizing for using such harsh words with him and he responded texting, "Every night I go to bed in my mom's apartment with a picture of our family looking at me. Last night I looked at you in the picture after processing all you had said to me, the names you called me, and how you said it and all I could think was I love her. I'm sorry that things unfolded this way but I'm not the monster you think I am and I'm not 'choosing' to hurt you."

I shook my head in disbelief. My heart ached for him. I wanted to help him. I was still watching him throw everything out the window and it hurt me and I hurt for him.

Chapter 6

Starting to Find My Way

My daily prayer was to take away my sadness, heal my heart, give me peace and happiness back, restore Jason's mind, fix our marriage and to make my children happy and whole.

The new school year came around and the children were not in school because Jason was, so called, homeschooling them. At that time, I wanted them to return to their school because nothing around them was normal. Jason and I were not normal, their home was not normal and on most days they were asking questions about us. I wanted them to go back to school so that they could at least have some type of normalcy and not think about us and interact with their friends on a regular basis.

Jason didn't want them to go because the school was getting really pricey and he wanted them to go to his school for free. The problem with that was that he only had two children at his school, and neither of them were the ages of Joi or Reese. We went back and forth about this subject on almost a daily basis until one day in early October I was finally able to convince Jason that the children should go to their old school.

I was sitting in my car in the parking lot of Walgreens under a shade tree. I anticipated this conversation being long and loud so I braced myself. After about ten minutes of me reiterating the reasons why it would be best for them, he said yes. I quickly got off the phone with him before he could change his mind and then I sent Eric and Kris a text to let them know the great news.

I began to cry as I formed the message to them because I was so full of emotion. I looked up to the heavens and said thank you as tears fell from my eyes. And then I couldn't stop thanking Him. My children could finally have an outlet to be carefree. That's all that I wanted for them.

That was a pivotal moment and the beginning of my healing. I had spent many days worrying about them and whether or not they were going to be ok. Joi cried a lot and was always asking questions about us and if we would get back together and why we had to be apart. Reese was showing his emotions by having outbursts of anger. I knew that if they returned to school then they would feel better, Joi wouldn't be so anxious and Reese would not be as angry.

I cried so much that day because I felt like my babies would be ok and I could finally stop worrying so much about them. And as the weeks passed I realized that because they were ok, I was ok. Tears stopped falling from my eyes, the anger started to lessen and I became focused on how to increase my income so that money would never be an issue in our lives and so that I could finally be the stay at home mother that I always wanted to be. And because I was doing so well, I didn't want to disturb my good vibes by serving divorce papers. I was fine where we were and figured I'd get to the papers some other time until the first weekend of November happened.

The children were staying with Jason for the weekend. My niece and nephew were in town with Rennie and Jason was trying to coordinate a time for Joi and Reese to meet up with them. He and Sasha had been texting for the last hour when a picture of Jason and Tina came through. Following the picture was the text, "enjoying the poly life."

I can only image the fright that went through him when he realized that he'd sent the message to Sasha. He instantly sent a follow up text saying, "Please disregard. That text wasn't meant for you. Please call me if you have any questions."

Have any questions? He was shook and was hopeful that I never found out but Rennie told me the next week. Even though I already suspected a relationship between them, I was still slightly shocked and angered. My intuition was right and that was what I needed to finalize the divorce papers.

Several weeks later I finished filling out the paperwork and on the Monday before Thanksgiving I had them notarized at the UPS store. All day I was happy to get the ball rolling on the divorce so I wasn't prepared at all for the emotions that were about to come. After leaving the UPS store a wave of sadness and anger jumped on me. This was all so surreal. As I drove home I replayed in my mind, as if it were currently happening, all of the foolishness that led up to this moment. I thought about the crazy love that I had for him and how much I wanted him to return. I wanted him to call and tell me that he couldn't live without me in his life. I wanted him to say that he made a mistake and to please forgive him. I wanted to embrace him and tell him that I wanted to work this out. I wanted to be the biggest thing in his world. I was enjoying the freedom that came with being single but I didn't want that freedom. I just wanted the man that I married but I had to accept that he was long gone. The man that I married no longer existed.

I had not shed a tear in over a month but on this day, I cried and cried and cried. And then I became enraged again. How did we get here? The words still stung when he said he didn't know if staying with me or being divorced but having his freedom was worse. I was deeply wounded. Those words were imprinted in my memory forever.

When I arrived home he was already there with the children. Even though I'd gone through those range of emotions, I didn't want to hurt him when I handed him the papers. I began to get nervous as I thought about how I would give them to him. The papers were in a manilla envelope so I figured I didn't have to tell him what it was. All I had to do was hand it to him. And I did just that. He told the children goodbye and walked out the garage door. I followed behind him and before he could reach the lock pad to put the garage door back down I called his name, "Jason."

He turned around with a curious look on his face. I had not looked him in his face in months but I felt like out of respect I could at least look at him for this. "Here," I said as I handed him the thick envelope.

He reached out his hand and said, "Thank you."

I didn't respond because I knew that if he knew what was in there he would not be thanking me. So, I just nodded and walked back into the house. Whew! My heart was aching.

155

Three days later it was Thanksgiving. I was sitting on the steps in the kitchen as the children ate breakfast. Reese was eating the pancakes I prepared at their request and the next thing I know, he got angry and threw the plate of pancakes and syrup on the floor. I saw red and snatched him out of the chair by his arm. I put his face close to the mess and scolded him. I then let go of him and told him to clean it up and don't ever throw the food that I prepared for him ever again. I was only inches away from his face and spoke through clenched teeth, "Do you understand me?!"

"Yes, Mommy."

I gripped his arm up again and said, "Now clean it up!" as I thrust his arm forward and let it go.

I sat back on the stair angrily. I knew I was wrong for getting on him like that. I directed my anger for his father towards him. "Where the fuck is his father?" I asked myself. I knew where he was though. He was supposed to be with them but decided he wanted to drive to Philly instead.

On a typical Thanksgiving Day, we would have eaten breakfast together and then gone to my parent's house and been amongst family for the entire day. So why am I sitting here on

Thanksgiving Day dealing with this shit by myself? I started to shake. If I'm going to hurt, you're going to hurt too I thought to myself as my fingers started typing a nasty text message to him. Five lines into the text Tosha called.

I had no pleasantries for her, "This is not a good day! I'm sending a scathing text! I'll send it to you when I'm done!" She uttered something like ok and then my fingers got back to typing.

[I've come to the realization today that I'm on the fence between an intense dislike for you and actual hatred for you. We built a life together and produced 3 children out of it. I stepped into this marriage having your back on everything. Anything in life that you ever wanted to pursue, I backed. I believed in you and stood up for you. I was your rock and you were mine. And then you started questioning the world and everything about it. And that ruined our marriage. You started to question why people should be monogamous and then you made a VERY selfish decision. You actually CHOSE other women (I don't care what you call it) over OUR family. You walked out, I put you out, whatever, on not only me, but our children. You decided that it was best for our children to grow up in a single parent household so that you could pursue freedom. You decided that if I couldn't get on board with sharing you then you will just bounce on me. You're a terrible person! Ultimately you left your children for women and freedom. You made a very selfish decision to choose yourself over your children. And you can't understand why I won't at least be your friend and how your best friend can just act like you never existed. You are no friend to me. Because my friend and husband would never do the things that you did. You shitted on our family! You would always talk about how well others co-parented. Now I realize why that was such a big thing to you. You have been thinking about getting out of this marriage longer then I actually realized. I hate you. Everything about you. But I'm thankful for being able to find a strength inside of me that I never knew I had. I'm thankful for my resilience. I'm thankful that I'm able to handle any and everything that life throws my way. I'm thankful for my children. I'm thankful for the lessons that I have learned. So, if nothing else, thank you for those things.]

Send.

"If I'm going to suffer, you're going to suffer too," I thought. But almost immediately after I sent it, I felt relief and sadness. I knew it was wrong to tell him I hated him even though at the moment I did.

I walked up the stairs leaving the children to themselves. I entered my bedroom, then the bathroom and then the closet.

Closing all three doors behind me. On the floor I sat, my back up against the door and I cried. I cried and cried and cried. I was so broken and I just couldn't understand how Jason could do this to our family. I played Kesha's 'Praying'. I sang and I cried. Gut wrenching crying. The tears wouldn't stop.

"...cause you brought the flames and you put me through hell, I had to learn how to fight for myself and we both know all the truth I can tell. I'll just say this as I wish you farewell. I hope you're somewhere praying. I hope your soul is changing. I hope you find your peace falling on your knees. Praying...cause I can make it on my own. I don't need you I found a strength I've never known...Sometimes I pray for you at night. Someday that maybe you'll see the light..."

I played the song over and over and every time I sang the words, "Some say in life you're gonna get what you give but some things only God can forgive," the sobbing would become more intense. Only God could forgive him for this because I didn't know how I could ever find it in my shattered heart to forgive him.

Eventually Reese came into the bathroom and said, "Mommy are you ok?"

I answered quickly with little words so that he couldn't here the gloom in my voice. "Yes. I'll be there in a minute."

"Ok!" And he left.

I realized at that moment that my butt was almost numb from sitting on the floor for close to an hour and a half. I was surprised that it took them that long to check on me. I suppose they knew that I needed some time away but my heart was touched when he came to check on me.

Several minutes later he was back asking the same question.

"Just give me a minute." I said as I stood up. I walked out the closet rubbing my backside after he left and I looked in the mirror at my face. My eyes were bloodshot red and my face was covered with tear stains. I just stood there wondering why Jason and I were not together. My lips started to frown and tears began to fall out of my eyes again. I just watched them fall until there were no more left. Then I took a shower to give my eyes time to heal and it was time to get back to mothering.

The big event that the Love's always looked forward to was just a day away. I started a tradition when Joi was just a baby to have Christmas Eve brunch at our home with all of our family and closest friends. As Christmas started to near this year she wanted to make sure we would still have the Love's annual Christmas brunch. So, if for no other reason, I had to prepare another fabulous brunch just for her, despite how I may be feeling.

I was shredding cheese for my famous macaroni and cheese, the sweet potato soufflé was ready to go in the oven, chicken wings were marinating in the fridge and the air was filled with sugar cookies mixed with Christmas tree scented candles. Christmas music had been blaring all morning as I sang to just about every song that came on. Some of the songs like "Silent Night" by The Temptations I had to stop and give my full attention to as I attempted to reach those high notes. My heart was happy as I thought about the house filling with my favorite people on Christmas Eve.

Jason always tended to the children while I prepared but this year Mimi took his place. In the midst of my preparations, she dropped by with the children. I turned the music down when they came inside to greet me and then they ran outdoors to play with the neighbors. Mimi and I started recounting all that had taken place since our separation. She was sharing how proud she was of me for being able to move forward with the brunch in spite of, and how I was able to move out of that dark place that I was once in only several months back. As we were talking a song caught my attention. It was a song by Jennifer Hudson that I'd never heard before named "Fix Me Jesus". As we were talking I tried to listen to the words and told myself I'd listen to it again when she left.

About an hour later she and the children left, several hours of cooking and preparing passed by, the kitchen was cleaned and the house was set up for about 40 guests, my back and feet were on fire and all of the food was finally prepared for Christmas Eve. I was exhausted but emotionally I felt really good. I went into my bathroom to wind down and remembered the song "Fix Me Jesus." I began to think about Jason as I listened to JHud wail out, "...fix me Jesus, oh fix me, fix me right now..." I knew that what Jason wanted was not of him. I knew that this was so much deeper than wanting to build relationships with other women. I knew that the lifestyle he was asking for had all to do with his past and nothing to do with his present. At this point, I no longer wanted to be married to him. I didn't know this new Jason and I was greatly anticipating the divorce but I did want my life back with the Jason that I'd married eleven and a half years ago.

As I listened to the words I started to think of all the ways that He fixed me. I spent endless hours crying and pleading for Him to help me. So many sleepless nights praying and thinking and crying. So many days of uncertainty. Months of endless anxiety. Sixteen pounds of weight loss. Uncontrolled and unpredictable crying outburst. And now here I was, standing strong, tall and confident. Knowing that I would be ok. Knowing that my children will be ok. I had an even more incredible love for my children that I'd never felt before this. I developed deeper friendships. I was so thankful and grateful.

I started to shed tears of joy as I recounted all of the ways that He fixed me. My feet were aching so I sat on the bathroom floor and kept replaying and singing "Fix Me Jesus." And then I started to thank Him. My back was against the wall, knees bent and my arms raised high as tears streamed down my face and I repeated, "Thank you," over and over.

I wanted to tell the friends that had been there from the beginning how thankful I was for them. I sent them individual texts saying, "As I prepare for this year's brunch I can't help to think about all of the people that care so freaking much about me and my babies. It literally moves me to tears. Thank you sooooooo much for everything. I cannot tell you how much I appreciate you!"

After sending the first few texts my eyes were so blurry that I couldn't see the print on the phone. My nose began to run. I was so thankful for my children, my parents, Mimi and my friends. It felt so good to cry tears of joy and gratefulness instead of tears of sorrow.

On Christmas day it was very important to Joi that Jason would be with them. So, when the children came into my room around the 8 o'clock hour full of excitement, the first thing I did was send Jason a text to let him know the children were ready for him to come over.

As we waited for Jason, Mimi and Drew to arrive, I prepared breakfast from the brunch leftovers. The Christmas tree scented candles were lit, Christmas tree lights were on and Christmas music played once again. This time on low volume. I anxiously anticipated this day because I wasn't quite sure how I would feel for our first Christmas in separate homes. But I felt good. Happy.

Once they arrived we started opening gifts and carrying on with our tradition of me sliding the gifts across the carpet to their rightful owners. As usual, Jason and I had to tell Reese to slow down and actually look at the gift after ripping the paper off before tearing the paper off of the next gift.

I didn't feel any tension in the air and everyone was happy. Jason and I only exchanged a handful of words but it was ok. All of us were laughing at the children's expressions of delight as they got exactly what they had asked for. This is what I had hoped for and it turned out much better than I had expected. After all of the gifts were opened we ate breakfast, had lots of desserts and played with all of the new toys and gadgets. Mimi made her rounds of calls to family members and put them on speaker so we could all shout out, "Merry Christmas!" Just like the years past. For me, this was actually one of our best Christmas'.

That night I received an email from Jason with pictures from earlier in the day. There were many pictures of Joi and Reese but to my surprise, there were pictures of just me enjoying myself. I thought that was very interesting. He still wanted to be with me. After all of the hateful things that I'd said in the past and he still wanted to be with me. I couldn't understand it.

And so the next day was even more surprising. He sent me another email. This one really blew me away. It read, "I know that you don't care about my feelings but I care about yours. And I'm concerned that you're going to meet someone who isn't going to respect you enough to be honest like me. Vanessa, I don't know any man who hasn't or wouldn't cheat under the right circumstances. The chances of finding a truly monogamous person is so slim. Let alone one who you get along with, one who communicates with you, and who you enjoy being friends with.

So yes, I am salty and envious of these other lying men. And more importantly I'm still in love with you and I don't want to see you invest in a guy like this in the future only to get disappointed and hurt.

I recently met an honest guy like me and his wife stayed with him, even though she's monogamous because in his words "she loves being with him and wants him to be happy and because he makes her happy".

I also met a different woman who is monogamous but is staying with her husband and trying an open relationship because she sees it as an opportunity for personal growth and because she knows her husband truly loves her and wants to be with her. She shared that it was initially heart breaking and it's hard for her but she's willing to try.

Again, yes I'm salty and envious when I hear these stories and it really hits home for me that maybe I didn't really make you as happy as I thought I did. I guess our relationship wasn't as great as it appeared on the surface and you really do see more value in breaking free from me than staying with me.

Otherwise you either believe the fairytale or don't realize that most people are already sharing their spouses and lie about it or you're not willing to go through the growth needed to make us work at this time.

And if that's the case then I'll always hold out hope till the day I die that you'll one day realize that we're in this position only because I DO love and respect you SO MUCH that I actually told you the truth about something that is a reality for most all people.

We don't have to end Vanessa...or maybe we do because you've decided I'm just the not the guy you want to grow with. Because trust me...the next guy will require you to grow through this and more as well.

I love you, I miss my best friend, and I want you to be happy with or without me."

I must admit, that email had me real messed up. I started to think that maybe I made the wrong decision. Maybe he was right and I will never find another man who will treat me the way that I want to be treated and one that I love as deeply as I loved Jason.

I was not only messed up but I was also annoyed, sad, angry and bothered. I was doing really well and then he threw this shit into my conscious.

The children were supposed to be with Jason for New Year's Eve. Being away from them was very difficult for me because all four of us were always together for the New Year. We would allow the children to stay up past midnight as we ate junk food all night, watched the New Year's Eve festivities on television and laughed, danced and loved on each other. So, I just had to accept that this is part of splitting up a family. We had to share the children separately.

I made sure I was not going to be alone that night. Tosha invited me over to her sister, Yvette's house. Her family was very fun loving and lively so I knew I'd have a good time there.

I was excited about what the New Year would bring and nervous about going into 2018 without my children. I started to get dressed for my outing around the nine o'clock hour. I blared the music to set the mood right. After showering I put on "Sorry Not Sorry" by Demi Lovato. "...Now I'm out here looking like revenge, feeling like a ten, the best I ever been, and yeah, I know how bad it must hurt to see me like this, but it gets worse (wait a minute). Now you're out here looking like regret, ain't too proud to beg, second chance you'll never get…"

I was bobbing hard to the lyrics as I stretched out my arms and waved both of my hands to the chorus, "…baby I'm sorry (I'm not sorry)…"

"…and yeah, I know you thought you had bigger, better things, bet right now this stings (wait a minute) 'cause the grass is greener under me, bright as technicolor, I can tell that you can see, and yeah, I know how bad it must hurt to see me like this…"

I was still bobbing and stepping. I had not put one article of clothing on yet and then my favorite part came on. I pointed my finger in the mirror as if I was pointing at Jason, "…talk that talk, baby, better walk, better walk that walk, baby, if you talk, if you talk that talk, baby, better walk, better walk that walk, baby, oh yeah…"

I could have performed in the mirror all night but it was time to get dressed and bring in the New Year.

Yvette's house was jumping from the moment that I walked in the door. Her daughter was in the middle of a circle of young ladies that were all having a dance off. Yvette was being a perfect hostess making sure that everyone was fed, had plenty of libations and ensuring that everyone was happy. When she spotted me she gave me a long warm hug. She always gave the best hugs. Her husband came over and hugged me too and asked how I was doing. He wasn't asking to make small talk. He sincerely wanted to know that I was ok because he knew that this was a rough time for me. Tosha gave me a hug and told me to have a seat and so that's what I did.

The house was so full of happiness and warmth. Everyone was mingling and enjoying the dance off that lasted for at least 30 minutes. I sat back and took in the scenery as I reflected on the last six months.

The clock was nearing midnight and glasses of champagne were being handed out. I started to get nervous because I didn't know what type of reaction I would have once the ball dropped. Would I start crying in front of all of these people? Vulnerability definitely wasn't my strong suite so I was hoping to suck back the tears if they should come.

"...59, 58, 57..." the countdown began.

I called Joi on facetime. My hand shook and my underarms started to perspire as the phone rang. Keep it together I told myself. The phone stopped ringing and there was lots of commotion on the receiving end. I started to count down as I held my phone up so that she and Reese could see me and all of the people in the room. "...5, 4, 3, 2, 1! Happy New Year! I love you baby! I love you son!"

"Love you Mommy! Happy New Year!"

I did it! The ball dropped but the tears didn't. I was a little choked up but I'll take that any day over all of the tears. My babies were happy. So, I was happy.

New Year's morning I woke up and responded to Jason's email that was sent the week prior.

"I actually gave you a free pass to have sex with someone else. I said I would have grace and work through it with you. But that wasn't enough for you. You had to have it all.

This isn't about your honesty. It's about you actually wanting to act on it. All of the trusted men that I have talked to and the women agree that just about every man would cheat if they wouldn't get caught/could live with themselves/were able to keep it as a secret/were in the wrong place at the wrong time. But these same men don't desire to break up their marriage for meaningless sex. So they avoid situations that can cause them to be weak. Some win. Some lose. But every man is not trying to be what you speak of nor do they want to be.

And to suggest that our relationship must not have been as great as it appeared and that you must not have made me happy is a bunch of nonsensical BS. I don't think this is necessary to say but I'll say it just one last time so that you are clear. I LOVED!!!!!!!!!! our marriage. I ALWAYS tell people that I had a beautiful marriage for 11 years. I would do it all over again but with a little more wisdom. Either way, I'd redo all 11 years with you.

Here's the problem that you refuse to understand about Vanessa. I'm NOT those other women. I'm not afraid to be by myself. I'm not afraid to be a single mother. I'm not afraid to do this by myself. And I WILL NOT sacrifice my happiness for yours. Marriage is about us making each other happy. Not about one spouse only making the other happy.

You do a whole lot of research and talk to different people like you and that are for people like you. You should try doing research about people like me that won't stand for that. My experiences are very different from yours. I'll share some. 1) A friend told me through tears that she wishes she was as strong as I am. She wishes she had of left but she was afraid to be a single mom and do this on her own. 2) A friend's sister stayed with her spouse who wanted what you're asking for. She insisted no but he pursued other women anyway. He also brought home a baby AND THEN she said no more. 3) A friend's best friend was married many years and dealt with overt cheating but was afraid to leave. She didn't want to be alone. She sacrificed herself. Eventually she couldn't take it any longer and left. After some time she realized that she is strong enough. 4) A friend's friend is currently with her husband and she portrays happiness. No one knows that she is dying inside but is afraid to leave for fear of being alone.

Do you get my point???? These women that you speak of are sacrificing their happiness to one day wake up like those women. They are putting themselves to the side. Many of the women that you speak of will not remain married. Either way, they are not me. I didn't want to be without you but it damn sure beat not having a peace of mind.

I have literally been to HELL face first. Do you hear me?!?!?!?!?! I didn't know how I was going to make it. My very best friend, the man that I was to die with one day decided he needed to be free of the marriage he signed up for. I didn't sign up for what you're asking for. I saw myself slowly dying because of the insurmountable stress that I was under. Many times I could

173

barely function. And if it wasn't for my babies at my side, and the strength that He gave me, I would not have made it. YOU JUST DON'T UNDERSTAND WHAT YOU PUT ME THROUGH AND WHAT I'VE BEEN THROUGH!!!!!!!!!!!!!!

You bounced on us. Reese needed you. He was slipping away and you bounced to save yourself. What if he never got back on track????? What if I never got back on track????? Then what?!?!?!?!?! Joi needed you!!!!!!!!!! You are selfish to leave us the way you did!!!!!!!!! You don't show the level of care and love for me or my children that I need you to. You only cared about yourself. We are now irreparable.

Here's what I was envious of when I did research. The man JUST like you that also had to make a choice. He chose his wife. His life with his family outweighed everything else. He could not see himself without her. On the other hand, you cannot see yourself without this other lifestyle. No thank you. We are over.

And this journey with you ABSOLUTELY requires growth. And I have grown in SO many incredible ways. I am so very proud of myself. I am more than capable! I am AMAZING!!!!!! I am TRULY AMAZING!!!!!!!! Who would have known that this is where I would land??? You should be proud."

After I hit send I felt a sense of relief. I wanted him to know what I'd been going through without yelling it down his throat. I was as clear as I could be and I was finally at the point where I no longer wanted him to change his mind because I no longer wanted him. I wanted the man that I'd married 11 years ago, not this counterfeit version of him. I suppose I still had love for him somewhere tucked away deep in a crevice of my heart but I no longer liked him.

Several weeks before divorce court I heard crying coming from Joi's room. "What's wrong baby?" I asked.

"I miss Daddy," she said between sniffles.

I put my arm around her, pulled her close and said, "I know baby."

"I don't like when you invite Mimi, Uncle Drew and Daddy's friends here and Daddy can't come over," she said.

I tried to be empathetic saying, "I understand baby but Mommy and Daddy don't make each other happy. Would you want me to invite people here that don't make you happy?"

She just sat with her head hung down. I repeated the question, "Would you?"

"I don't know," she answered.

"You do know baby. You wouldn't want someone around here that doesn't make you happy," I said.

"Well I don't like the way you're handling this. You said you would make this comfortable for me and I'm not comfortable," she boldly stated.

These conversations with her always aggravated me because I couldn't tell her the truth. Many times, I wanted to say, "Screw your father. He's the cause of this." But I told myself that I would never give them a reason not to like their father so I would always try to be patient.

But this time it hurt. I know she looks at me like I'm the bad one because he walks around being sad that everyone is upset with him. She feels that and takes it on and tends to try and defend and protect him.

The next day I couldn't shake that feeling and I was at work in Lisa's office again, behind closed doors with tears falling from my eyes. This was so unfair.

Chapter 7

The Divorce

My alarm went off and I popped up out of bed like it was the morning of my wedding. The night before my heart tried to back out of divorce court but my mind wouldn't let it. I was so afraid. I didn't know what to expect. Was I going to have to stand before a jury? Was I going to be asked personal questions in front of strangers? Was I going to start crying? What if they didn't grant me the divorce?

The only thing that I knew for certain was that Jason would not be there. Two days back I asked him if he finished the parenting class. He told me that he wasn't going to take it and that he wasn't going to be present.

"Why?" I asked very annoyed but quietly. Reese was there and I didn't want to get myself riled up.

Calmly Jason responded, "I read that if I don't show up you can still proceed with it."

"Just be calm Vanessa," I told myself.

"Well can you at least complete the parenting class? It doesn't take long and it says in the paperwork that it must be completed by both parties," I spoke very softly.

I was so angry. I just wanted him to comply. I didn't want anything to hold this divorce up.

"No, I'm not...'

"Jason. Can you please just do that? I don't want to have to go back just because of that," I cut him off. I was clearly very irritated by this point.

"I don't want to make you any more upset than you already are Vanessa. If you can give me a reason to do it then I will but I don't think I have to," he said sticking to his guns.

I let out a deep breath of annoyance, put my hands up as to surrender and said, "Forget it. Just forget it. Don't worry about it."

So, other than knowing he wouldn't be there, I had no idea what to expect.

The children had school so Mimi came over to get them ready so that I could focus on what was yet to come.

I prepared the same way that I prepared for my wedding. I shaved all body parts and made sure I looked my best. Even though Jason wasn't going be there, I still wanted to look good. I wore a black v-neck cashmere-like sweater with silver earrings about the size of a half dollar with a pattern similar to the texture of wood grains. Fitted blue jeans and black stiletto boots were on my bottom half. I may have been scared as hell but I was cute.

As I made my way through the traffic to court I thought about how relaxed I was. My nerves had finally left me and I was ready to sit before a judge. I started to think something was emotionally wrong with me because I was so calm.

There was an hour to spare when I drove into a parking spot. So, I just sat there and thought about what was about to happen next. I was emotional but no tears fell until Tosha's text came through. It read, "Good morning! I know today is going to seem like a really hard day but just remember that it is only going to get better from here. You are closing a chapter of your life to start an even better one!!! Call me if you need to talk or if you need ANYTHING!!!"

My eyes began to weep again. My emotions ran free every time I thought about how supportive my friends had been. I sat there for about twenty more minutes and pulled myself together.

Forty-five minutes passed as I sat on the hardwood bench inside the courtroom waiting for my name to be called. My underarms were sweating but the rest of my body was chilly. It was a strange and uncomfortable feeling. "Love," the courtroom attendant called out as she looked around waiting for a hand to raise.

She was standing right next to me. "Yes," I answered softly.

She noticed me and then continued to look around the courtroom. I didn't know what to call him so I said, "Jason Love is not here."

"Ok. Its protocol for me to call his name outside the courtroom too," she said.

After she came back in she walked me to the judge's chambers where I took a seat at a long wooden table. The table sat between ten and twelve people but at this moment there was only me in the middle of the long end, the attendant two seats to the left of me and the judge to my right at the head of the table. The room was rather small, well-lit and very empty. The walls were a pale shade of green without any pictures hanging. Other than chairs,

180

the table and us three, the only other thing in the room was the judge's laptop, a printer and an open box of tissue.

She asked me some clarifying questions and then I was sworn in. Raise your right hand and state your full name. "Here we go," I thought to myself.

"Vanessa Love," I answered.

Next question asked was, "What was the date of your marriage?"

My eyes became blurry and a lump appeared in my throat. I didn't want to answer the question. I never thought that question would cause so much pain. I took a long pause and a deep breath while choking back the tears and answered, "May 5, 2006."

Damn! This was really real. She asked some more questions and then printed out the final paperwork. "File these downstairs with the clerk," she said as she handed me the final judgement and decree papers.

As I walked to the clerk I read the papers. "...It is considered, ordered and decreed by this court that the marriage contract heretofore entered into between the parties to this case, from and after this date, be and is set aside and dissolved as fully and effectually as if no such contract had ever been made or entered into…"

Damn! Reading that paragraph was so unfair. I thought to myself, "They are acting as though my marriage never existed." That paragraph was so powerful and hurtful. My eyes began to blur again but I held back the tears long enough to file the papers.

I walked out of the building with my head hung low. When I realized my head was hanging I told myself, "Hold your head up high."

And so I did. I walked with my head held high, eyes full of tears and heartbroken.

Jace met me for a late breakfast immediately following court. She waited by her car while I parked. She stood about five foot one with a very petite frame. Her beautifully wide smile revealed perfectly straight white teeth that always made her eyes light up. She was beautiful with perfect hershey colored skin. Her head was clean shaven and she stood with a stance of confidence and no nonsense. She understood what I had been going through because she was separated and recently started the divorce process.

When I got out the car she greeted me with a warm smile and a long tight hug. Then we walked to the restaurant with her arm around my waist and my arm around her shoulder. We sat across the table from each other and she asked, "How are you feeling?"

I just looked at her. I wasn't sure how I felt. She put her hand on the table for me to hold. I held her hand and smiled. That was such a beautiful gesture. I thought some more about how I felt. "I have to use the bathroom," I said.

As I went to the bathroom I asked myself, "how do you feel?"

When I returned to the table I said, "I feel like this is the stupidest thing I've ever heard of!"

"How so?" she asked.

"It just blows my f-ing mind that we are divorced because he wants to date other women and build relationships and have sex with them. He wants to take women on dates," I said shaking my head back and forth.

We sat for two hours and covered a variety of topics such as dating, future financial plans, starting over and sex. We laughed more than anything else. It was refreshing to laugh after such a pivotal morning.

After parting I went to the park that I had spent countless hours at over the past seven months. This was the park that I sat at as I screamed for the entire park to hear that I was divorcing him. I recalled a time that I was at work, showing my "pretend face." My emotions were getting the best of me and I could hardly hold the tears any longer. I walked down the long hospital halls that seemed never ending on that day. I told myself, "You're almost there. Hold it in." My eyeballs were almost popping trying to keep the tears from falling. And as I was about twenty-five feet away from the car the first tear fell. I held my head low and walked as fast as I could as the flood gates opened. I felt so relieved when I put my hand on the door handle. I flopped down in the seat, closed the door behind me and rested my head on the steering wheel. I began to sob uncontrollably. The car echoed my pain as the sounds of agony got louder. I just wanted to get to the park so that I could sit and think.

I cried just about all thirty minutes to get there, as I vigorously wiped away the tears. By the time I arrived my sleeves were damp from all of the tears that had fallen. I walked until I got to the dock. I took a seat and leaned up against the post and admired the view. The lake was merkey but nonetheless, the scene was beautiful. The water was surrounded by tall trees with thick green leaves and strong trunks. The sky had thin scattered clouds. Evening was falling so the sun wasn't high and the temperature was perfect after being inside with air conditioning all day. There were two couples with children, each with a dog, on the other side of the dock. The children laughed loudly as they played with the dogs and the parents mingled with each other. The scene was so perfect and touched my heart so deeply that I was reminded of the very reason why I sat on the dock all alone. The sobbing started again. It was gut wrenching and I didn't try to stop it this time. I prayed out loud and asked God for wisdom, peace and understanding.

After sitting for almost two hours, I decided it was time to go home and see my babies. I was hopeful that Jason would not be there. As I walked towards the entrance of the park, alongside the fence that bordered the trees, I felt the heaviness of the reality weighing me down. I felt like I had not prayed enough and if only I prayed more, asked for more, praised more, than I could get relief. And then the song "Can't Give Up Now" by Mary Mary came to me. I stuck my ear buds in my ears and started listening to "...Lord I know that you didn't bring me out here just to leave me lonely, even when I can't see clearly, I know that you are with me so I just can't give up now cause I've come to far from where I've started from, nobody told me the road would be easy and I don't believe he's brought me this far to leave me..."

I raised my hands to the heavens and dropped to my knees. I felt the words so deeply in my soul that my body started heaving as I sang the words through the sobbing. I began to praise the Lord as I sang the words. "Thank you for never leaving me. Thank you Lord...."

I bent over and rested my face on my hands in the grass. I didn't even think about the people watching me. All I cared about was getting my husband back and restoring my family. I wanted my children to be whole and happy. I wanted them to have a life of normalcy. I wanted to be happy with my best friend again. So I prayed out loud for those things with my face down. And then I sat up and raised my hands again and repeated, "Thank you Lord," until the sobbing stopped.

Today the sky was perfectly blue without a cloud in sight. The trees were almost barren of leaves but the trunks still looked just as strong. The air was crisp and the sun's rays were warm but the breeze made the air chilly. This day was so final and poignant. It was unfair that Jason didn't have to go through the motions that I had to experience. There was a strong desire for me to share my feelings with him and so as I sat on the bench swing under one of the trees, I wrote a thoughtful email and sent it to him.

"I'm not sure where to start. May 5, 2006 was the happiest day of my life next to the birth of Joi and Reese. I married my perfect mate. We were equally yoked and I could not wait to start my new life with you. I loved you with the deepest parts of my soul. We made so many beautiful memories together. We had each other's back. I was truly your ride or die chick. We faced tragedy together and survived. Our children had a stable and loving home.

You changed. Which is ok because people change. But you went backwards. You became adolescent like, only thinking about yourself. Your children and I were no longer a priority. You become focused on your needs only and tried to make me feel bad by saying I don't love you unconditionally. Well guess what....giving me the ultimatum of polygamy or nothing is a condition.

You are weak. Honest, but weak nonetheless. You are not emotionally equipped to hold down our family. You let the world get between us. Women of unknown origin got between us. Sex and lust. And when Reese was crashing, those things were more important. They were more important then me and Joi. They were more important than our family life. What we built. What we shared. Our dreams. You became more important than us.

You are a coward. You were too afraid to even witness the dissolution of our marriage today. Too afraid to appear in court. And if this is "who you are" why keep secrets and be so concerned about who knows. Our marriage wasn't a secret so why should your new lifestyle be one.

For me, my children come first and so I will always do what's best for them. And what is best for them, and me, is for me to have forgiveness towards you. I'm in no way in a place of forgiveness right now. But for my babies and my best future I will strive towards that.

Thank you for 11 years and my 3 babies. I felt loved and loved deeply.

January 23, 2018. A New Year!

Ms. Vanessa Love"

After sending the email I texted everyone that mattered to let them know that the divorce was final. I was sad and disappointed. I thought I was going to be happy after court because I could finally move forward in my new life. But instead, I was just very blah. Not overly emotional, just blah. I stared at the blue sky and just marveled at what I had been through over the past seven months. I was so proud of myself for dragging myself out of hell. I recognized that if not for the strength, resilience, bounce back and fortitude that God made me with, I would still be in hell. My mind flashed back to the panic attacks, uncontrollable fits of crying, counseling sessions with Jason, and sitting at different parks for hours on end trying to figure this all out. And then I started to think about my babies. I focused on moving forward because, in my mind, Jason could leave them for good so I was the only one guaranteed to stay by their sides. I loved them more than anything in this world and I had to make sure they would be ok. I wanted them to always feel loved and happy. A smile came across my face as I thought about Joi and Reese and I thanked God for saving me.

I thought back to a time in November, shortly before Thanksgiving, when the children were with Jason for the weekend. I was cleaning my house on Saturday morning. I had not stepped outside yet but the sun was shining bright and it looked as though it was warm outside. I felt at ease that day. I had music playing in the background and I was in the children's bathroom cleaning the tub. I was thinking about the new life that I was living and all of the ways in which I was finally doing better. And then something totally unexpected happened inside of me. I looked up and said, "Thank you Jesus." I finally wasn't asking to keep my old life but instead I was saying thank you for my new one. I was thanking God for allowing me to be more than ok. I was not only paying the bills, but I was also able to save money, and spend money on me and the children. I was doing great and I was finally thankful. At that moment I realized that God didn't answer the prayer of keeping my marriage together but he did answer the prayer of making me whole again and being emotionally stable for my children. And they were also happy. And I was thankful.

So, as I sat I continued to reminisce and listen to all of the songs that were so meaningful to me over the last seven months. And then I spoke out loud, "It's over now. I did it." I was so proud of myself.

And then I listened to Kirk Franklin's "The Storm is Over Now". The words could not be more fitting "...no more cloudy days, they're all gone away, I feel like I can make it the storm is over now. If I walk alone, I'm not on my own, I feel like I can make it, the storm is over now.... No more crying at night, the storm is over now... no more tears and sorrow, no more heartache and pain, no more suffering, no more, it's over now..."

After two location changes, shifting my position to find comfort at first on the bench and then on the tree roots that I sat on as I leaned against a mighty tree trunk, and three and a half hours later, I decided it was time to eat. On my way driving to one of my favorite seafood restaurants I called Calin to say thank you for her listening ear and her wisdom. I had not sat in her office since October and on that day, I told her that I would start the divorce process. Needless to say, she was shocked to see that only three months later, the divorce was finalized. During the conversation in route to the restaurant, she left me with some more words of wisdom and she told me that the healing process from a divorce is about two years. "Two years!" I exclaimed.

I put that information in the front of my brain so that for the next two years if I started to feel down I would remember that it's ok. But I must admit, that bit of information got me down a little.

Next, I called Mimi. I was so thankful for so many people and so many things that my heart wanted to sing. I told her that the divorce was final and that I was doing ok. And then I opened up her floodgates of tears when I said, "Mimi, I want you to know that when I get married again I will have two mother in laws. My new husband will have to embrace not only my children and my parents but you as well. You are part of the package."

She began to cry and tell me how much that meant to her. Her relationship with Jason was almost nonexistent. Even though he

191

lived with her, he did not converse with her other than the common pleasantries like hi and bye. She was thankful that she truly gained another daughter out of our marriage and that I would not leave her side because of him.

After my conversation with her I called my parents and thanked them for all that they had done for me and my children during the last seven months. The conversation didn't last long because I was becoming famished.

While I sat by myself I looked around at the neighboring tables and wondered what their stories were. What were they going through? I understood that you never know what someone is going through unless they tell you. We all needed to be kind to each other because you never know when you may have the chance to be the highlight of someone's day.

By now it was 8:30 and time to head home but not before I ended the night with something cold to make my emotions happy. I drove to my friends TCBY on Hwy 85 and ordered my favorite frozen yogurt, vanilla caramel. I sat in the car and pushed the seat all the way back and put my feet on the dashboard as I sat in the car and ate in silence. I could only hear my thoughts as I recapped the day. I pulled back the sunroof visor so that I could look at the starry night. I gazed at the moon and wondered what

Jason was doing. I wondered what he did that day and was he ok.

I thought about the range of emotions that I felt for him over the past seven months. On some days I wanted him to never return. I thought it would be best if he just died. On other days I would weep for him because I knew he was hurting. I was watching my husband and best friend destroy his life. I would hurt for him. I wanted to help him. I wanted his mind to be restored. I wanted him to seek counseling and learn about how his past helped shape his new idea of marriage. Still, on other days I would have an intense hatred for him and want to pulverize him. But on this day, January 23, I just wanted him to be ok.

My eyes started to get heavy and I needed to see my children. Every since Jason moved out they would not go to sleep until I returned home, no matter what time it was. So, sure enough, when I walked through the door at 9:30 on a school night, there they were, running to me and saying my name with jubilation.

I greeted Mimi as Joi asked, "How was your day Mommy?"

"Interesting," I answered.

"What was so interesting about it?' She inquired.

I took a deep breath and said, "Eh. I'll tell you about it some other time. Let's go to bed. I'm exhausted."

I knew she would not ask me again in the morning.

After putting them to bed I started to lay my head down on the pillow and then I decided that I could not go to sleep without documenting the day. So, I wrote in my journal and at 10:30 that night I ended the entry with "Good night to my New Year! Watch me live 2018!"

The next day I woke up feeling pretty good. I got the children ready for school and after returning home from dropping them off at school I made myself some pancakes and eggs and had a seat on the couch. I had a massage and spa outing set up for later that day and so I decided to just relax until then. About two hours had passed in front of mindless television watching and I decided to take a nap. I started to climb into bed and then the garage door started to open. No sooner then it opened, it was shut. And then Jason sent a text saying, "Didn't know you were home."

I had a crazed look of shock on my face as I stared at the text. "Oh no! This isn't happening. This is my house now," I said out loud.

And then I fired out an email. Respectfully I asked that he not come to my home if I'm not there and unannounced. I couldn't wait for the divorce to be final so that I could tell him that he could no longer wash his clothes there and so I included that in the email and then asked that he only watch the children at his mom's apartment. I ended the email stating that I'm not trying to be nasty or offensive but that we both need to move on and heal and the current situation of us still sharing space is not helpful or healthy for either of us.

Then I told myself not to check my email until the next day because I didn't want to ruin my spa experience. I was so fired up that I just laid there until it was time to leave for the spa.

The masseuse opened the door to a tranquil room. It had the smell of aromatherapy and peace. The lights were very dim and I could see steam rising where the lamp sat. The room appeared to be a shade of light blue and it had pictures hanging of oceans and mountains, and sunsets. All of nature's beauty. As picturesque as the room was, all I wanted to do was lay face down on the warm white sheets so when she told me to remove my clothes to my comfort level and lay down on the table, I started to take my shirt off before she had a chance to close the door behind her.

I'm pretty sure that massage was the most relaxing seventy-five minutes I'd ever experienced. Next, I sat in the steam room for 15 minutes. After about the first seven minutes I started to ask myself why I felt the need to sit for another eight minutes. I was damn near dying in the heat but I figured, like all other aspects of my life, if someone else is able to sit in that scorching heat for fifteen minutes then so am I. So, I watch the sandglass as the minutes slipped away in sand granules.

To end my spa experience, I got a glass of champagne and some light snacks and sat on the bench in the roomy one-person shower stall. I watched the water fall and sipped on my glass of champagne. I thought to myself, "This is the life." I wanted to frequent the spa more often and just live life. I imagined myself happy beyond belief, traveling the world with my children at my side. We were going to have a great life. A fulfilling life. Yesterday was only the beginning.

As I stood to wash my body I realized that I was tipsy. I wasn't a big drinker. In fact, if I really wanted to, I could probably count how many drinks I had in an entire year. So needless to say, it didn't take much to alter my senses.

I started to smile and laugh at myself. I was so happy and, strange as it sounds, it felt free to be tipsy in the middle of the day. After

I got dressed I decided to walk to my dinner destination because I wasn't going to make it safely by car. Through blurry gazed eyes I looked at the front desk attendant and asked, "What's good to eat around here?"

He gave me several options and I started to walk my happy butt to one of his suggestions. As I was walking I texted a few girlfriends saying, "I'm tipsy and I like it." I was so tickled with myself. Life was good.

The next day I checked my email and there was no response from Jason. I felt like I didn't know much of him anymore but what I did know was this, he was not going to let me slide with that email that I sent. And so two days later on Friday it started with a phone call when I was relaxing on the couch that we used to snuggle up on together.

"Hello," I answered. Since I was working towards forgiveness I figured I should also answer his phone calls.

After hello he stated, "I want you to know that I don't agree to those terms about my access to the house. I'm rarely there when no one is there and when I am I don't go into your space. If you want to discuss selling so you can get your own space let me know."

"I am not going to sell the house. Unfortunate for both of us, divorce sucks big time. Nothing about it feels good. Everything changes and we have to find a new way to move forward. The house is not shared property anymore. The divorce papers says the property is awarded to the petitioner. I am not trying to be hurtful. This is part of the change that comes with divorce," I said.

Angrily he responded saying, "I'll have to read that in the papers. We may be going back to court then. I literally never come by there unless I stop by to work for an hour or so before picking up the kids from school while I wash clothes. And that's rare. You expect me to help you by picking up the kids on weekdays but I can't even wash clothes or watch the kids there? Not happening!"

I'm thinking, "Go back to court? You didn't go to court remember?" And didn't he want to be free? It sounded to me like he wanted to be free while I still provided life's conveniences like a place to wash his clothes. What did he think would happen? Like he said, not happening!

Nonetheless, I responded calmly, "You washed your clothes and hung out here while we were separated. And you did those things without an issue from me. We were separated, not divorced. I know it's hard to wrap your mind around that. It's hard for me wrap my head around it too. We are not separated anymore."

I went on to say, "If you do not want to pick the children up after school anymore, just let me know. Me asking you to help out with our children should have nothing to do with the aforementioned issue. We are both going to need help. We should come together when it involves them. And it also benefits you because you can spend more time with them. But like I said, if you don't want to help, just let me know."

He was fired up now and said, "If I watch the children it will be at the house. If you don't want me to watch them there then you'll have to find another way. I don't see how me being there when you're not makes things uncomfortable for your healing. I also should be able to wash my clothes there while I'm with my kids until I get my own place. How is that a burden to you?"

By now I was getting aggravated but calmly I said, "Saying 'I'm divorced' out loud stings like a bitch. But that's now my reality and I know that I have to move forward. It's really, really, really difficult to do that when you are still around. I don't want you washing your clothes at the house or watching the children at the house because it feels like we are still connected. We are divorced. And although you don't understand how my healing is connected to my requests, you just have to understand that's my process. More importantly, we are divorced. That means you have a home that you share with the children and I have my home that I share with the children. I cannot discuss this anymore with you so I'm hanging up now. Goodbye."

I was so confused as to what he thought was going to happen. Several days before court he asked me if I took him off of my health insurance. I screwed my face up to the question because again, what did he think would happen? That became the most puzzling question amongst my circle during the last seven months. What did he think would happen?

Later that evening he called back. I looked at the phone with annoyance as I contemplated whether or not I should answer it. "Hello?" I answered with a question in my voice.

He started with, "Hopefully I can say this for the last time. I'm tired of you twisting my intent and hurling hateful rhetoric towards me whenever you feel like. Self-preservation is not the same as selfishness. I tried to fight against myself for many years and it made me unhealthy. I revealed myself to you and asked you to accept me as I am. You declined and that was your right. You said you could not live in an open marriage and I could not live in a closed one. We both hated those feelings. So why are you having such a hard time understanding me? You asked me to leave the marriage so stop twisting things to blame me for leaving. The fact is neither of us are to blame. Stop it with the blame and the guilt. There is nothing wrong with me and I deserve to be loved and treated with respect. You know nothing about unconditional love and I seriously question if you ever loved me or if you were just in love with the idea of me, a husband."

Here we go again. I don't know why I even entertained the conversation because at this point it no longer mattered but I couldn't let him go on saying those things without a response so with deep thought I responded, "Jason, as much as I don't understand you, you don't understand me. And that drives me crazy just like it drives you crazy. If you truly understood how I feel you would 100% understand why I say and do things that I do. I am hurting! And I don't understand how you can choose that lifestyle over what we had. "

I went on to say, "If I only liked the idea of you then I wouldn't care about any of this. Your feelings wouldn't be hurt because I would be out of your life peacefully. I'm not sure how you have come to that conclusion but if you knew how I felt then you wouldn't question what I say or do."

"You don't know what it felt like to sit in front of the judge and be asked to, 'state the date of your marriage.' You didn't have to answer that question or have to choke back the tears and answer it. You didn't have to read the words in that divorce decree and walk them downstairs to be filed while your eyes were full of tears. You didn't have to do that."

By now my voice was shaking. "I did. You don't know the feeling of being too afraid to go to court but going anyway. That's my experience. And so yes, I called you a coward. I'm sorry if that was hurtful but that's how I feel. It was a coward move."

There was silence on the other end and I looked at the phone to make sure he was still there. He was and so I continued. "My mind is f'ing blown that the last seven months even happened. Not because I loved the idea of you, but because I actually loved you, liked you and was in deep love with you. I loved seeing you walk through the garage door and answering your phone calls, dating you, making love to you, cooking delicious meals for you, looking at you, going on vacations with you. You get me? And believe if you want that I don't know unconditional love but when you really start to understand how I feel, how my heart aches because you needed a different lifestyle, how I prayed and cried and pleaded and sobbed and endured, then you will understand how much I actually did want you and the intense love that I had for you. No one goes through all of that just for an idea. I'm actually confused as to how you think I should respond to my husband needing and wanting to share himself with other women. My feelings are crushed and you can't tell me how to feel or respond."

He was a much better listener than me. I would have never let him get that much out without interrupting him. I can't stand listening to the bullshit that he tells me but at this point I figured why not let him say his last peace because this was the last conversation that I was ever willing to have with him about this.

So, I subjected myself to what would be the final words that I was willing to hear as he said, "I'm having a hard time understanding how you can say "you can't tell me how to feel' or 'you don't know how hard this is' when that is exactly what you've been doing to me. You refuse to accept that people are and can be polyamorous and that is me and how I was born. You treated me like I would actually try to hurt you on purpose and that it's not possible for people to make it work when in reality many do. You've never taken ownership for the fact that you chose to leave me. You chose to divorce me. I didn't want to leave."

And with that my blood started to boil. He says that like I woke up one morning deciding to get divorced. He tried to change the vows under which we got married and then expected me to go along with his foolishness. Every time he spoke of 'how he was born' instead of acknowledging how his upbringing shaped his ideas, my patience thinned out.

He continued to say, "The main reason you are bitter is because you still think I did something to you. It has nothing to do with you. I asked you to accept me as I am so that I can feel like a whole person and you said, 'no.' I was hurting and I wasn't happy because monogamy was unnatural for me. You had every right to say no but stop walking around playing the victim and casting blame when in reality we were both equally hurt by my self-discovery. Tell it like it really is."

I could listen to no more and shouted, "Truce! I'm done!"

And almost with the last word he said, "Ok. Truce. Just know that it's equally hurtful for me to accept that you couldn't accept me as I am especially when I know so many couples who made it work. I pray that you gain broader understanding of this situation in time. It's not about you and you're taking it so personal."

I let out a lifeless, "Whatever Jason. I hope you make it out of this ok," and hung up the phone.

Chapter 8

New Year, New Me

This new life that I was living wasn't bad at all. I had the freedom to do whatever I wanted, however and whenever I wanted without having to consider another adult. I was in charge of all of the financial decisions and I sure wasn't suffering financially. The freedom of not having to consider another person in my financial purchases was priceless.

Three weeks after the divorce I went to see Mary J. Blige in concert. I'm almost certain that if I was still married there would have been a great possibility that I would not have been able to go see her. I thought about these factors as I drove to meet Jace, Tosha and Misty at the restaurant before the main event.

The ladies were dressed super cute. Jace was dressed very simple but elegant with a black blouse and a white cardigan across her shoulders. Her heels were white with black polka dots on them to compliment her outfit and she held a small red handbag. Perfect and elegant. I always admired her style.

Tosha had a chill but "I'm fly" look going on. She wore a funky black leather jacket with black patterned boots that her ripped up jeans fell over. Around her neck were spikes and her faux locks were pinned up perfectly.

Misty's face was flawless with her hair pinned up and long baby doll curls hanging on both sides. She was blessed in ways that I wasn't and she wore it well. If I had her tatas I'd have them hanging out all of the time. Today she had them fully covered with a long necklace that lay perfectly in between. Very sexy.

I wore a pair of very fitted blue jeans and a simple black sweater blouse and cute brown boots that probably didn't really go with the outfit. My girls looked dope and I was plain. I told myself never again will I not be just as fly as the company that I was with.

The ladies ordered bottles of tasty wine while I had just a glass of Chardonnay. They all teased me for being a lightweight. There was lots of girl talk but what really stood out to me was a comment that Misty made. I was talking about what dating would be like for me and all of my standards that had to be met. She said, "What's with all of these rules? You always have rules. You need to just live in the moment. If you want to do something, do it. If you don't, don't. But stop with the rules. Shit!"

She was really feeling her wine but I got her point. I was going to just live in the moment. Just be free.

There was a corny local rapper that opened up for Mary so as we waited we talked about all of the songs that we hoped she'd sing. And then the crowd exploded and the entire theatre stood to their feet. As she graced the stage she was dancing like I do in the mirror at home. She made us feel like she was one of the girls, dancing hard in the mirror to our favorite songs. She wore a big yellow bomber coat with black leather pants and black stilettos. She ran through all of her classics, "Love Without a Limit," "Real Love," "You Remind Me." Tosha sat to my right and Jace sat next to her. She danced past Tosha to bump butts with both of us as she sang "Just Fine."

We danced hard and sang loud. Standing to my left, Misty was in her own world. It was like she was alone in her home dancing in the mirror. Every once in a while, she would turn to me and tell me how amazing the concert was.

Then Mary sang "Not Gon' Cry" and she spoke to my heart. Jace's too. We both leaned across Tosha's lap as we vibed and passionately sang the words, "...I know there are no guarantees, in love you take your chances, but somehow it seems unfair to me, look at the circumstances, through sickness and health 'till death do us part, those were the words that we said from our hearts, so now when you say that your leaving me, I don't get that part... helping you get on your feet, eleven years of sacrifice, and you can leave me at the drop of a dime, swallowed my fears, stood by your side...well I'm not gon cry, I'm not gon cry, I'm not gon shed no tears, No, I'm not gon cry, It's not the time, 'cause your not worth my tears..."

Those words were so powerful to me. Eleven years! And all gone because of these women. Damn!

Then Mary started to talk about her own marriage and all of the disaster that it caused. She said, "...there's a special place in Hell for assholes like you..." And the theatre exploded again.

I leaned to Tosha, "Yo! Did she just say there's a special place in Hell for assholes like you?!"

And then I asked Jace. And then I leaned to my left and said to Misty, "Yo! Did you hear what she said?!"

At that moment I felt like Mary was preaching because that's exactly how I felt.

The concert was nearing the end and then came "No More Drama." "...it feels so good when you let go, avoid the drama in your life, now you're free from all the pain, free from all the game, free from all the stress, so buy your happiness, I don't know, only God knows where the story ends for me, but I know where the story begins, It's up to us to choose, whether we win or lose, and I choose to win…"

She sang the hell out of that song and then she did what I often felt like. She dropped to the floor. Layed out. Done! She was over it. She removed the hat from her head and just breathed. No more drama!

I had a conversation in early December with Kris about celebrating my divorce with all of my friends that supported me through it. My friends were such an intricate part of helping me heal that I had to celebrate making it out of hell with them. They were my therapy. Sometimes I would talk to them for hours. Sometimes multiple times a day and they never knew which Vanessa they were going to get. Would they get the happy, I'm good, Vanessa? The vexed Vanessa. The crying Vanessa. The confused Vanessa. The sad Vanessa. The, I'm excited to see all of the possibilities Vanessa. The filthy mouth Vanessa. The anxious Vanessa. The hyper because I see my way out of this Vanessa.

They never knew which one they were going to get but they never stopped answering my phone calls. They never knew how long I was going to keep them on the phone but they still answered my phone calls. They never knew if I was going to tell the same story that I'd already told them ten times before but they still answered the phone. And they never knew how many versions of me they would get in one phone call but they still answered the phone.

My heart would always swell with love every time I thought about in how many ways I loved and appreciated them so I could not see finalizing this divorce without them. I was so excited to go out with them for my divorce celebration but after the divorce was final I wasn't in any mood to celebrate. I was so sad that I couldn't even set a date for the celebration. I realized that there is no celebration in divorce. I did not get married to celebrate my divorce. But there was a celebration in me finding new life. And so I called it a "celebration of life." And a week after the divorce was final, I was ready to celebrate life with my girls.

Six weeks after my 'New Year' began, in early March, six of my nine closest friends came together all on the account of me. I wanted to look super cute this time. I wore a teal, fashionably holey shirt that draped slightly off my shoulders and showed the little bit of cleavage that I had. My blue jeans were very fitted and my feet were covered with milk chocolate colored and slightly worn knee high boots. My eyebrows were freshly arched and the curls on my head were popping. My silver earrings dangled alongside my beautiful and full of life countenance.

The first stop was my house. I layed out white party plates with gold bubbles on them, matching napkins and gold forks. Each girlfriend had a thank you card with thoughtful words of appreciation in them. I prepared for them my exceptionally delicious wings, perfectly broiled shrimp and for the meatless eaters, meatless meatballs. Brownies go great with everything so I made that and of course, we had to toast with champagne in gold glittered champagne flutes.

Before the toast I thanked each of them and looked them individually in their eyes and told them how much I appreciated them and that I will always have their back, no matter what. And I meant that.

Then we Ubered to a place called "Escape the Room" where we spent an hour trying to find clues to get out of a room that we voluntarily got locked in. It was great watching all of their personalities come out and mesh together. Some of them just sat back and watched while others were adamant about finding the key and getting us out of there. It was fun and the best part for me was watching all of them laugh and be true to their personalities.

We then ended our night at a soulful urban cafe. There was a live soul and R&B band playing who complimented the cafe's urban feel. The walls were mustard colored with colorful abstract pictures on them. We sat at a long counter height black marbled table that rested between two brick wall structures.

As soon as we were seated we ordered drinks and the conversation got to flowing. My spirit was so full being around my favorite people as they flowed from one conversation to the next. My friends were all living different lives. They consisted of being married, divorced, widowed, a fiancé and me. So the conversation got interesting when opinions started about men, marriage and dating. Denise struck a chord when she gave her divorced view of men. She tapped on Tosha's plate with half eaten pizza and jokingly but seriously asked, "Who wants to eat this pizza every day for the rest of their life?"

I understood her point but marriage was different and I think the married women felt the same way. To me, marriage and sex was bigger than eating a meal but I understood where she was coming from.

"I hear you Denise and I believe that no man or woman wants to eat the same dish but for some, it's not worth rocking a perfectly happy marriage for a moment of pleasure," I answered.

Even though I was divorced I still believed in love and marriage. I refuse to believe that all men are that weak that given the perfect marriage for them, because nothing is perfect, they would screw it up for just a moment of pleasure.

Some more thoughts went around the table about the subject matter and where interrupted when I heard the leader of the band announce, "We got Vanessa in the house tonight having a celebration of life."

I threw my hands up and yelled out a cheerful, "Yeah boy!"

My face was beaming as I picked out the culprit and said to Misty, "Oh man! That's what you were doing over there."

She smiled and I said, "That's what's up. Thank you." Again, my heart was gleaming.

More topics bounced around the table and we started talking about should a woman ask a man out on a date. Jace said she would. I wasn't in disagreement with her but I just couldn't see

214

myself asking out a man. I didn't have the nerve and I responded by saying, "I'm not asking a man out."

Then Misty, who's married, put in her two cents about my rules, "Here you go with your rules again Vanessa. Stop with the rules. If you see someone that you like, ask him out. So what." The New York in her always came out when she was drinking and I loved it.

I breathed hard and laughed while saying, "Leave me alone."

We parted after a few hours of fun girl talk, great music in our ears and memories that I would forever cherish. The four of us Ubered back to my home while the rest of the ladies parted their own ways. Tosha sat in the front seat and played DJ. It was about midnight and I was still full of fuel. I danced in my seat to every song she played and then she put on Beyonce's, Shining and said, "Y'all don't know nothin bout this young bucs."

"Man, I know this," I said as I rattled off all of the words.

When we returned home and the night ended, my ears were filled with silence and my heart was spilling of overflow. Thank God for great friends.

My birthday was quickly approaching and all I could think about was not wanting to be in Jason's presence on my day since Joi and I shared the same birthday. I didn't want him to miss her celebration so I had to find a way to be ok with him being around on my day also. I also thought about the ridiculousness that occurred only six weeks after I turned 40. I realized over the past few months that although Jason did want to give me a birthday to remember, he also timed the events perfectly. He thought that if he went all out for my birthday and showed me how much he loved me then I would be more apt to go along with his idea of polyamory. I started to realize that there were many events during our marriage that were just subtle setups for his benefit.

I recalled the time when we owned an older Dodge. I didn't like anything about that car and eventually it didn't even have air conditioning. Jason was teaching third grade at a nearby school at the time. He had convinced me that I should drive the Dodge as opposed to the Honda Accord which was newer and in better condition. His rationale was that because I drove further to work, I should drive the car that was better on gas to save money. I didn't want to drive it but he convinced me that it was best for our budget.

I had a 60-mile commute to and from work every day and I had convinced myself that I was doing what was best for our household. But the other side of me knew a husband should not have his wife driving around in an older, not as reliable car. The spring time came around and we learned that the air conditioning didn't work. Driving to work was fine but coming home was like an infirmary in the height of the Georgia heat. At the time my hair was long and pressed out. I would drive home with a scrunchy in my hair so that it wouldn't get too wet from perspiration. I always jumped in the shower when I arrived home because I would reek of sweat. I was so thankful for the rainy days although sometimes that was difficult too but it would be so humid that rolling the windows down would only make me more uncomfortable.

One day it was over 100 degrees outside and I couldn't drive fast enough to get home and jump out the car to tell Jason that I'm never driving in that car again. He protested saying that the gas would throw off the budget but I told him I don't care about a budget. So instead he drove the car for a few weeks to work about five miles away. He would return home with his clothes drenched. Shortly after, we purchased another car.

This time it was a Grand Am. I didn't like that one either but it sure beat the Dodge. I felt better about driving that one but I still preferred the Honda Accord. One day I was driving home from work and it stalled on the highway. Luckily, I was able to make it to the shoulder. I called Jason to tell him what happened as I sat on the side of the road waiting for triple A. I wasn't annoyed because stuff happens. No big deal. Until the second time about a month later.

I sat on the side of the road again. This time very irritated. I told Jason that we must figure out why this keeps happening because I don't want to be on the side of the road again. You would think that at that point he would offer to drive the car so that I would not have to be stranded again. But that didn't happen.

The third time I had Joi and Reese in the car. Reese was still a baby and sitting in a rear faced position in his car seat. Smoke started to rise out of the hood. I pulled over in an apartment complex and I got my babies out of the car as fast I could. We moved far away because I didn't know if an explosion would be next. I called him again and this time I was hot. "I'm not driving this car anymore!" I sternly stated.

"I'll take it into the shop," he calmly said.

"You can do whatever you want but I'm not driving it," I reiterated.

"We will talk about it tonight," he said.

I was ready for that conversation because I wasn't sitting in the driver's seat not another day.

Later that evening Jason tried to convince me that we could get it fixed and it will be fine. "I am not driving that car anymore. You can get it fixed and then drive it. But tomorrow morning and every day after that I'm driving the Accord. You can do what you want with the Grand Am," I stated my final word.

Jason drove the car for maybe a week and then decided that we needed a new car. But before we got rid of it and bought a nice Acura he asked me to take a picture of him in front of it. He said, "I will use this picture when we make it to show what I was driving before."

I snapped the picture but I was annoyed because I knew that only my butt sat in the driver's seat. Why would he portray that he struggled like that?

This is one of several like-stories that I thought about as I approached 41. He knew that he could convince me of anything as long as he gave me a good rational reason and always showed me love. I knew he loved me. That was never a question but also I realized that he manipulated many situations to go in his favor. I realized that I'd never told him no in 11 years but if I ever I did say no about something that was important enough to him, then our marriage would have ended before this. My 40th birthday party was another part of his sincere love for me and his manipulation.

So as 41 approached my mind was fixed on the partial manipulation of my marriage and on the simple fact that I didn't have anyone to make a big deal out of my birthday this year. I was talking to my good friend Denise one day and I told her just that, "Man. I don't have a husband this year so there's no one to make a big deal out of my birthday."

She said with conviction, "You make a big deal out of your own birthday. You have a lot of good friends around you. Do something together with them."

It's funny because when I was single before Jason, I always made a big deal out of my day. I celebrated everything and loved going out and having people over my house for social gatherings. She was right. I'll throw my own party. I didn't need anyone to do it for me.

I took two weeks off from work because I simply needed a break and I never worked on or near my birthday anyway. Four days before my day I went to the spa. Whenever I'd get a massage I never wanted to get off the table. I wanted to lay there until the next morning. So, this time, I went to a spa that was inside of a hotel where I spent the night. I figured I'd treat myself. I more than deserved it after the year I'd had.

After the massage and spa treatment I sat at the hotel terrace restaurant. It felt so good, freeing, to be out on my own and enjoying life. I was free to come and go as I pleased. As I waited for my meal, I began to think back on what I'd been through.

Ten and a half months ago I was broken both physically and emotionally. I was afraid of what the future held for both me and my children. I couldn't see myself without Jason and the future that I expected to have with him.

My world crashed but I knew that somehow, I would pull myself out of despair. I believed that I had enough fortitude to withstand all of the pain in order to save myself and be the mother that my children needed.

In allowing myself to be vulnerable, something that I was very uncomfortable with, I was able to lean on the shoulders of my parents, Mimi and my friends. I shed buckets of tears, some of which I let them see and hear. And in that, I was able to gain strength and a positive outlook on the future.

I'd forgotten who I was and what I was capable of. Before marriage I was a young woman that was full of life and no one could convince me that there was anything that I couldn't do. I accomplished all things that I set my mind to.

I never lost that during my union with Jason but I did put my success in his hands. I waited for him to make our dreams of financial freedom and traveling the world and leaving a legacy for our children come true.

Now it's my turn and I'm up for the challenge. I'm enjoying carving out a path for myself and my children. I'm proud of myself for all that I have accomplished up until this moment and I get giddy about what I'm creating for the future.

I know that my story will touch many women's lives and give them courage to live their best life, however that may look. I hope that as I share my story, other women will see a glimpse of themselves and realize that they are capable of not only making tough life decisions but also surviving the consequences of those decisions.

I never felt encaged in my marriage but I will say that this new freedom is amazing and I'm enjoying all aspects of it. My next hurdle to overcome is forgiveness because I know that when I have forgiven Jason, I will truly be free.

I was loved deeply and I loved deeply for 11 years. Many people will never experience that type of love and so I am grateful for my marriage. Maya Angelou said it best, "First best is falling in love. Second best is being in love. Least best is falling out of love. But any of it is better than never having been in love."

My reflections were interrupted by my tasty crab cake burger followed by a quiet evening in the hotel room watching a movie on a king sized super comfy mattress.

The next night was my birthday gathering with friends. I wore an Easter colored green dress. The sleeves were three quarter length and the dress stopped right about my knees. It was a sheer flowy material that accentuated the curves that I did have. I wore silver bracelets on both wrists and a silver, black and gold thin intertwined rope-like necklace that rested between my breasts. I was going for the look that Misty had during the Mary J. Blige concert but I guess I actually needed to have bigger tatas for that. Anyhow, I was cute nonetheless. My fingernails and toenails were polished a matching color green and I wore black stilettos pumps.

The curls in my hair were perfect and I was definitely feeling myself. I was cute and ready to start another year of life.

I was touched to see twelve of my friends, some new and some old, come together on the account of me. I made sure I sat in the middle of the table so that I could hear all of the conversations. I wanted to soak in a little bit of everyone. I found myself dipping and dabbing into everyone's conversations as they laughed, ate plenty and enjoyed one another's company.

I ordered a glass of chardonnay and sipped on it as I usually do. Misty joked with me again about the slow pace in which my drinks disappeared. Another friend, Erin, chimed in as she shared stories about me drinking in her home. I rarely had a drink but at Erin's home she always had something tasty waiting for me. All three of us had a good laugh about our drinking habits.

I was feeling everyone's good vibes and then the band caught our attention when they sang Prince's 'Purple Rain'. We swayed to the melody as we lifted our phones and waved our flashlights. We sang and a handful of us joined in with all out passion as we sang the words "…only want to see you walking in the purple rain, honey I know I know I know times are changing" and then I air fiddled playing the guitar. I was getting down and then we rocked back and forth with passion as we finished the song out crooning, "Ohhh ohhh ohhh ohhhh…"

For some reason that made me emotional. Just sitting amongst friends, acting silly, people laughing at my antics, drinks flowing, good food all around. So after the song went off I wanted to make a speech. But I first had to gather my emotions. I didn't want any tears. Just smiles and laughter.

But before I could say a word, Erin said, "Let's sing happy birthday."

And the table sang the traditional happy birthday song. Then she yelled out, "Remix!"

I joined them in singing Stevie Wonder's version of happy birthday. My cousin to my left laughed at me for singing along. What can I say? I had my full personality back and I wasn't ever going to hold back.

Before biting into my cake I spoke a few heartfelt words, "I want to thank every one of you for coming out to celebrate my birthday. You know I've been to hell and back this year and I'll be honest, I was a bit sad leading up to this day. I felt like I didn't have a husband to make my day a big deal. And then I said 'you know what' I'm gonna make this thing a big freaking deal. I'm gonna invite my friends out to celebrate with me. You all don't know how much this means to me. I thank you all from the bottom of my freaking heart. I don't want to cry so I'll stop but I thank you all so much."

They clapped and cheered and I felt loved. Just like I did a year ago.

When I returned home and laid my head on the pillow I thought about Joi and Reese. I thought about how much I loved and cherished them and how I was once so afraid for them. I fought for my marriage not only for my benefit but for theirs as well. I cried many tears for them and I prayed for them to be whole and happy. They are whole and happy and as I drifted off to sleep the soundtrack to my life, Andra Day's song, 'Rise Up', played in my head.

You're broken down and tired of living life on a merry go round.

And you can't find the fighter but I see it in you so we gonna walk it out and move mountains.

I'll rise up for you...

When the silence isn't quiet and it feels like it's getting hard to breath.

And I know you feel like dying but I promise we'll take the world to its feet and move mountains.

I'll rise unafraid for you...

All we need is hope. And for that we have each other. We will rise up.

I'll rise up. In spite of the ache. I will rise a thousand times again for you...

About the Author

Jennifer L. Speed lives in Georgia with her daughter and son. They are the loves of her life and she finds great joy in spending quality time with them. She is a lover of life and enjoys having a great laugh with friends, inspiring those around her and staying fit. She's been a pediatric nurse for 16 years and is pursuing inspirational speaking.

Made in the USA
Columbia, SC
14 November 2018